milk &
COOKIES

An Intimate Story about Rising Above
the Trauma of Sexual Abuse

STACEY KIRKPATRICK

First Edition

Copyright © 2022 Stacey Kirkpatrick
All rights reserved.

ISBN: 978-1-957124-03-2

Published by Kate Butler Books

All rights reserved. No part of this publication may be reproduced, stored in a retrieval system, or transmitted in any form or by any means, electronic, mechanical, photocopying, recording or other-wise, without prior written permission, except in brief quotation in critical articles and reviews.

Design by Margaret Cogswell
www.margaretcogswell.com

WHAT READERS ARE SAYING

"A must read for families who have a history of childhood sexual abuse, Stacey shares how she overcame her traumatic experience and her journey back to an empowered life."

Mike Vukelic, coach, speaker, and author of Let Go of the Sh*! Show and The Mind, The Muscle & The Miracle - A Survival Guide for Men How to Lead with Balance, Strength, and Certainty in a New World

"Hope. Strength. Love. Out of a secretly abusive life, Stacey Kirkpatrick comes through it and uses her experiences to help others to see what must be seen. We need to be aware of what is happening around us, especially around our children. Kirkpatrick helps us to be aware. A book written from her soul, it shows us to not be complacent for those in our care."

Margaret Kirkpatrick, Children's Librarian

"This book really moved me, and it's one you will think about long after you've turned the last page. Stacey has a way of writing that you feel every emotion. I feel this book will be a gift for so many who need a voice."

Nita Nichols, Yoga Instructor

"Having known Stacey for many years, she has always impressed me with her strength of character and generous nature. She has always been available to those in need and always with a smile and kind words. To now have read what she went through in her youth, the struggles and obstacles that could have easily derailed her life and lead her down a very different path, makes her current situation and outlook all the more impressive."

Lee Veary

"Milk and Cookies is an easy but difficult read—a whirlwind of emotion, to say the least. I wanted to stop reading when my eyes welled up too much to read on, or my anger began to rise into my chest. I also felt a strong responsibility to take this little girl's hand through her journey to be sure she made it through safely and that she found her happy ending."

Tara Adams

DEDICATION

I want to dedicate this book to my husband, who has always supported me. To my children who continually inspire me and push me to think beyond myself. To my mom who taught me how to be independent and gave me the strength and courage I needed to write this book. And to all the survivors out there. Know that you are not alone, and there is a path to healing.

TABLE OF CONTENTS

Prologue..9

Part 1 - Trauma..13

Part 2 - Consequence..63

Part 3 - Resolve..163

Epilogue...183

CONTENT WARNING

This book contains content about childhood sexual abuse, sexual assault, domestic violence, and suicide. Some readers may find this distressing or difficult to read. If you find yourself in crisis, please reach out to your local crisis support line, a therapist, family member or friend for support.

PROLOGUE

Mom was born in the early fifties, part of the Baby Boomers generation. She had a sister six years older and another six years younger than herself. She also had a brother, five years her senior. Another older brother died in his first year of life, likely from crib death, what we now call SIDS. I can't imagine the profound sadness my grandparents felt losing a child.

My grandfather flew for the Royal Canadian Air Force, and he married my grandmother, who was living in England. After the war, my grandfather brought his new bride to Canada. From the outside, the family appeared to be as many of that time. My grandparents worked hard and eventually saved enough to buy a house, a small bungalow, which they would live in until they died.

There are stories of my grandmother's various jobs, which as a child always seemed intriguing. She worked in the cafeteria in parliament, preparing lunch for the prime minister and other members of parliament. She woke early to head to another job baking fresh bread and cooking for the nuns who lived and taught at a local Catholic school. I had visions of fresh loaves of bread coming out of the oven, the glorious smell filling the room, imagining it was the best place in the world to have worked. She even held a position at the lavish Capital Theatre with its grand staircases to the balcony, a large crystal chandelier lighting the space, and velvet settees lining the walls. There was once mention of her working at the famous Prescott Hotel, back when it was still a hotel and ladies had to have escorts to be allowed in the dining room side and were forbidden from the pub side. Some of these stories I overheard as a child from tidbits of conversations. Later I asked about the memories, some of which had been long since forgotten. The main theme I can pull from these stories is how hard she worked to provide for her family.

Stories of my grandfather were mostly from his time in the war flying in a Lancaster. Later he worked for the Post Office, but there was little else shared. Every morning, he would read the local newspaper cover to cover, and every evening, he would watch the six o'clock news. Many years later, my mom would have some peculiar memories of him, memories that her therapist said had been repressed. Her telling of them was vague and uncertain, but to this day, I question if there wasn't a lot more to them—and more in alignment with my own.

Some of the stories of my mom's childhood shed a light that suggests things were not easy. Her older sister was kicked out of the house when she wanted to marry a man my grandparents did not approve of and her belongings were thrown onto the front lawn. Her youngest sister remembers not being allowed to sleep during the day and how she would have to hide in her closet to take a nap. Mom often shares the story of one Christmas when she was five or six, and there wasn't enough money for gifts. Her older siblings got nothing, and she alone was given a gift of crayons and a colouring book. It seems as though she continued to feel guilty for being the only one to get gifts that year.

My grandmother was very particular and liked things "just so." Another Christmas years later, she was in a mood as the house hadn't been cleaned well enough, or perhaps some other missteps had occurred. Mom had bought her boyfriend a record for

Christmas, and my grandmother smashed it. Mom had planned to drop it off later that day and recalls her tears over not having anything for her boyfriend. She fondly recalls her brother-in-law, the one my grandparents didn't approve of, giving her a cologne set so she would have a gift for her boyfriend. The stories suggest some level of dysfunction in the family that would play a part in my mom and her siblings' future lives. They have all had their challenges and struggled in their earlier relationships. The depth of that dysfunction is not discussed or perhaps not remembered. Some believe these things are better left unsaid.

    The story of the abuse my grandmother suffered includes her father sitting her on a stove and how she was later adopted by another family. My grandmother rarely ever spoke about any aspect of her early life, and I have never heard about her own mother. Thinking about mom's past, I see her in a different light today. She was a victim of emotional abuse and perhaps more from an early age. These are cycles that play out over and over, and I often wonder what my grandparents endured in their own lives that began in the mid-1920s and what my mom endured in the 1950s.

PART 1
trauma

chapter 1

It was probably 1977, and I was around four years old. Mom tucked me into bed and said goodnight. She walked out of the spare bedroom at her parents' house, and I heard the front door close. Mom and my grandmother headed off to their night shift at the post office, and I would spend the night with my grandfather. The bed linens were always fresh with the scent of laundry soap. The chill on the cool cotton sheets would barely be warmed by my body before I hopped out of bed. In my long flannel nightgown with small pink flowers, I went to the kitchen, where my grandfather sat drinking his tea. He pulled out a plate and took the lid off the cookie jar that sat at the end of the breakfast counter, and while I chose a few cookies, he poured me a glass of milk. This nightly ritual of milk and cookies was our little secret.

"Don't tell your mother," he said. I knew it was wrong. I was never allowed to get up after I had been put to bed at home, but this was our special secret, just between a grandfather and his granddaughter.

My grandparents hadn't shared a bedroom in years. My grandmother, who we all called Nanny, had a pretty room with a frilly white bedspread and lace-covered throw pillows. There were plastic flowers in white porcelain vases set on starched, crocheted doilies. Collectible figurines of ladies in fancy gowns sat on her dresser, and next to her bed, there was an old metal alarm clock with two bells at the top and a hammer that would release at the appointed time to clang the bells. In stark contrast, my grandfather had his man cave across the hall, although that term would not be used for another few decades. He had dark, heavy wood furniture, and the walls were covered with subdued tartan plaid wallpaper and prints of World War II aircraft. My grandfather proudly told me how he was a rear gunner in a Lancaster (WWII British heavy bomber) during the war, a very dangerous spot as other pilots would aim to take out the rear gunner, leaving the plane defenceless.

He had boxes of personal belongings placed on his shelves, next to neatly folded shirts. Nanny allowed him to keep some of his stuff, as long as it was organized and neatly put away. My favourite item in my grandfather's room was his short-wave radio. The body of the radio was covered in black leather, as radios often were in the seventies. On the nights that I wasn't tired, I would go into his room after milk and cookies and lift the flap in front of the radio to reveal a world map etched on metal. I turned the knobs and searched for a signal, often discovering foreign languages and unfamiliar music from far-off lands. It was like opening a portal to another world and getting to eavesdrop on other people's lives.

And our secret continued. Every night after my mom left, the milk and cookies would be ready for me, and I would begin my imaginary play. Some nights, I was an explorer as I listened to the radio. My grandfather would climb into bed while I played on his radio and talk with me, sometimes sharing stories, sometimes asking my opinion. One day he asked for help solving a problem.

"Sometimes, when I sleep, I have dreams, and when I wake up, there is a mess. You know how much your Nanny doesn't like a mess, so I need to figure out how to keep the sheets clean," he said. I didn't understand what he meant.

"What kind of mess?" I asked. He took me down to the bathroom, stood in front of the sink, and proceeded to masturbate so I would understand his problem.

"This happens when I have dreams at night, and then I have to wash the sheets, so Nanny doesn't know," he said. We went back to his room, and he pulled out a condom.

"If you put these over it, it catches everything," he said as he opened the package.

"Why don't you just put one on when you go to bed then?" I asked, thinking it seemed an obvious solution.

"It has to be firm for the condom to stay on. Can you help me put it on?" he asked as he laid down on his bed, stroking himself. He held the tip of the condom over his now firm penis and had me put my hands on him. I unrolled the condom, and he proceeded to masturbate again, taking his time and eventually ejaculating into the condom. At the age of four, I didn't know anything was wrong with this. I just knew that we couldn't tell anyone because they would know Grandpa was making a mess, and Nanny didn't like messes.

Other times, after milk and cookies, I would go to my grandparents' finished basement and play house. There was a refrigerator in one corner and a spare bedroom at the other end of the basement. The main living room area had two couches and a bar that I pretended was a kitchen. It was like my very own personal, full-sized playhouse. Behind the bar, in my "kitchen," I would use the cocktail shaker, strainer, bottle opener, and ice tongs to pretend I was cooking dinner. In my "living room," I would turn on the fake fireplace and watch the orange glow from the light that rotated behind the plastic logs. My grandfather sat on the couch; he was the daddy, and I was the mommy, just like on television. Sometimes, I turned off the lights so the mommy and daddy could go to sleep. I took off my clothes and would lie naked on my grandfather while he lay on the couch. I don't recall if he touched me.

"We shouldn't do this," he said with a gentle laugh.

One night after I had gone to bed, I awoke to the sound of the television, and I went out to see what my grandfather was watching. I stood in the hallway, looking at the television scenes as my grandfather sat in the dark room alone. He noticed me there and tapped the couch beside him, so I crawled up and watched. The movie had young teens at a private school who had sex with various staff members and other students. It was pornography, possibly child porn, although I cannot be certain. Anyone over fourteen would have looked like an adult to me at that age. My grandfather let me sit on the couch and watch the rest of the explicitly graphic movie. He didn't say a word, but I saw him looking over at me as I watched.

Our little secrets, the late-night games and movies, and the milk and cookies were all part of his grooming process. When people wonder why kids don't tell others about what is going on, it is because it starts out seemingly innocent. Sexual abuse isn't always a traumatic event that scares a child. It can start as something fun that the child enjoys. Sexual abuse also doesn't have to be about penetration. It can be any kind of inappropriate sexual behaviour. Abuse of any kind is about power and control. Without my realizing it, my grandfather had set in motion his control over me. He normalized sexual behaviour at a young age and made it seem like the secret was for my benefit. If I told, I might get in trouble for getting up when I was supposed to be sleeping. Also, I might not get to have milk and cookies anymore.

Even if I had known to tell my mom, it would have just added to her struggles as a single parent. With my grandfather retired, she had a free, trustworthy babysitter while she worked, plus she and Nanny worked together, so carpooling made perfect sense. Being a divorcée in the mid-seventies was still looked down upon, so it was astonishing that she dared to leave her abusive husband and get a job to support herself with a two-year-old toddler. She was only twenty-three when she left. Years later, she would tell me about her short-lived marriage to my dad. After she married him, they lived in a townhouse on the army base in the city. The fights had escalated, and she went to speak with the base chaplain, but all he did was suggest it was her fault.

"What did you do to make your husband mad?" Like anything a person could do would warrant hitting them, shoving them into walls, or pushing them down the stairs. My mom was brave during a time when women stayed in their marriage because society didn't accept divorced women. If the police were called, they would soon be gone because it was just a domestic dispute. When she left, we lived with my grandparents for a couple of months, then a series of apartments and a communal house with a few other adults for one summer.

I only saw my dad sporadically. There would be a long drive out to my dad's parents' house, and my daddy would be there. The house was originally just a cottage with a couple of small bedrooms and a kitchen that opened to a living room. Grandpa Norman had redwood lumber shipped across the country to add on to his little home, and the final product was the perfect log cabin complete with a large stone hearth. The old living room became a dining room with a long table that could seat the whole family, grandparents, children, and grandchildren. This felt like a magical place where we sat by the roaring fire or played in the cubby in Grandpa Norman's office with my cousins. The house looked out over the river, and I could sit for hours on the rocks at the water's edge, reading, and later, writing.

My dad's mom had died when he was eighteen, so I never knew my paternal grandmother. She had been sick for years, and there were stories that she was crazy, but it turned out she had a brain tumour. Dad had enlisted in the army right from high school and was away in Germany when they called him to come home. He was to come home before the end but waited a couple of days, and then he was too late. I often wondered if he did that on purpose so he didn't have to face her at the end. He was never very good with goodbyes.

Grandpa Norman remarried soon after to Ethel. They were together for as long as I could remember. One of the younger grandchildren couldn't say grandma, and it came out as "Ga." Somehow that stuck, but I always felt silly calling her Ga. I was in kindergarten, after all, and I didn't use baby words like Ga anymore. It was summer, and Ga invited the whole family to visit with my dad while he was on leave from his military posting. There were lawn chairs placed around the yard and a picnic lunch spread on the table. The grandchildren played in a blow-up kiddie pool while the adults sat around and enjoyed the sun and a drink or two. My dad loved his rum and coke.

Back then, my favourite toy was a Magic Slate. It was cardboard with plastic that I drew on and then could lift the plastic sheet, and it would magically disappear. As we dried in the sun after hours in the small pool, my dad drew cartoon characters on the Magic Slate, one after the other, and I was mesmerized by his amazing talent. Dad was this cool guy who could draw Mickey Mouse and Bugs Bunny. When I was with dad, I had fun. It was always a weekend of playing with cousins and spending time with family. My memories of visits with him were just little snippets of scenes like this, but nothing more.

Inevitably the visit would end, and dad would have to go back to base. With each visit, it seemed he was stationed farther and farther away as he was gradually posted farther across the country. One day, at the end of the visit, we drove my dad to a crossroads in what felt like the middle of nowhere. He was meeting up with one of his army buddies to catch a ride to wherever they were headed. We pulled over to the side of the road, the dust from the gravel filling the air. As we waited, the dust settled, and dad didn't say anything. Another car pulled up, and he hugged me goodbye. I hugged him back and began to cry. There, in the middle of the road, I clung to my father, not wanting him to leave again, but duty called. My aunt, who was with us, pulled me away, and he left quickly. He didn't say a word. He just left. No, "I love you," no "goodbye," not a word. I watched the car drive off into the distance, disappearing beyond the dust.

I grew up in Ottawa, and with few exceptions, have lived within fifteen miles of my childhood home. Ottawa is the capital of Canada and lies within a valley with a river running down the middle. Across the river, the terrain rises up into hills that are referred to as the Gatineau Hills, and they can be seen from several spots in the city. From almost any vantage point in Ottawa, those hills are only twenty to thirty minutes away across the bridges. As a child, I thought they were mountains because they rose so high. Of course, I was only four or five, and my perspective may have been a little off. When we would drive through the city and catch a glimpse of those hills, I would imagine my dad lived far away on the other side of the presumed mountains. After a long drive, I imagined that we could get to the other side and see my dad. In my mind, he always lived "just over there," just over the horizon, not understanding that he lived half a continent away.

My daddy left me again and again. He never stayed. He would send brown paper packages tied with string at Christmas and for my birthday. The gifts were the kind of things usually bought for someone you don't know. When I was younger, I received generic toys, never the ones I hoped Santa would bring. At ten years old, my gifts were a blow dryer and a year later, hot rollers so I could curl my hair. He never called of his own accord. Mom would call him, and I would bounce off the furniture while she spoke with him, telling him to talk to me.

"Maybe you can come to visit one day soon," he said, as he described living near the mountains that run along the west coast of Canada and down into the United States. "The chinook came through off the mountains and warmed things up so much that we were out on the back deck in shorts earlier, even though there's four feet of snow on the ground," he explained. "Maybe one day you could come live with us. You would like to have a pool, wouldn't you?" he asked. He made promises of a house with my own room, a pool, and I would get to eat candy because Daddy always let me have candy. "Wouldn't that be wonderful?" he said. As I got off the phone, I was delighted with the prospect of this new world.

"Dad's going to get me a pool and candy," I told my mom. But I didn't visit him, and I didn't get a house with a pool. I only got those packages that arrived by mail, wrapped in brown paper.

chapter 2

I only have brief snippets of memories of some of the places mom and I lived. At one point around 1976, we lived in a communal house in the Glebe, near downtown Ottawa. The Glebe was Ottawa's first suburb, full of grand old homes built in the late 1800s. Mom rented two rooms in that house on Third Avenue, sharing the space with several other renters. The front of the house had only a tiny lawn, and the steep front steps rose to the large veranda. The living room was just off to the side through the front door and had a large wood fireplace. The room was empty but for an old church pew right in the middle. A large kitchen was at the back, shared by all the renters. I climbed the stairs to the second level, then turned the corner to find another set of stairs to my bedroom, on the third level. Even though it was the attic, it was a very bright space, with wood plank floors and walls painted a pale pink. There was plenty of room for my toys in the very large room. The house was home to hippies and activists, including one I would later see on the news storming the House of Commons in the Canadian Parliament Building to make some radical statement. Today, he would probably have been shot during an attempt at such an act.

People seemed to come and go all the time. One of the residents called me over to the porch on the second floor.

"Do you want to see magic?" he asked.

"Yes," I said, eyes bright, looking down at the little brown beans in his hand. He placed the beans down in a sunny spot and waved his hands over them a few times.

"We need a little patience. Can you be patient?" he asked. I shook my head in the affirmative and stared down at the beans intently. Suddenly the beans started to move back and forth a little and then started to jump around. I was mesmerized.

"They're Mexican Jumping Beans," he told me. These were magic beans, I thought, like in Jack and the Beanstalk. Could fairy tales be real?

The house seemed full of mystery and adventure. In the bathroom, the old clawfoot bathtub sat inside a dark closet. It seemed a strange place for a bathtub but fit with the peculiar character of the house. When mom decided to give the bathroom a good clean, she found small plastic toy dishes under the tub and gave them to me to play with. I imagined them left behind by another child who lived there and wondered what had happened to them.

I sat on a blanket on the lawn for a picnic with my new toy dishes and picked grass seed to cook for lunch. A brother and sister lived next door, and they came over with a tricycle. I had never ridden a tricycle and walked over to the edge of the lawn. Being shy, I just watched them go back and forth on the sidewalk. The little girl brought the tricycle over to me as if to let me try. I didn't know what to do, so I stood on the back ledge and pushed it forward, unfortunately, right over the girl's toes. Her brother grabbed the trike from me.

"Leave my sister alone," he yelled at me. I started to cry and ran inside, ashamed I had hurt the little girl and scared because he seemed so mad.

Evenings we would sit on the church pew with a fire lit,

and the front living room would glow orange. People would share stories, and mom talked about the strange room in the basement, painted red from top to bottom. I wasn't allowed in the basement, and I imagined fascinating ghosts visiting us in the big, old house. Mom loved scary movies and said the house reminded her of the house in *Amityville Horror*. She also loved mystical and mysterious things, so ghosts and superstition were a normal part of the conversation.

Although most memories were just flashes, I experienced plenty for a house we only lived in for a few months. I remember Mom complaining about some of the residents throwing out her white sugar because they thought it was bad for her. I remember many skinned knees from falls on the sidewalk, and I remember the smell of popcorn and candy floss wafting down the street from the exhibition that came every year to the fairgrounds just a couple blocks away. It was a summer of innocence and simplicity.

My dad was in town that summer, and we had a few visits. Mom told me stories of when I would come home from seeing my dad and how I would stand in the middle of the large kitchen and scream at the top of my lungs and pee. Her housemates, of course, had all kinds of theories and recommendations, but none of them had children. I don't recall any of this. I was busy being a kid, playing, and having adventures.

After that summer, we moved into a one-bedroom apartment, right beside a tall building's main entrance. The bang of the main door would rattle the walls as people came and left the building at all times of the night. The apartment was tiny, and cockroaches scurried across the wall when I turned on the lights. The laundry room in the basement of the building was filthy, and the machines took hours to run and were often out of order. Mom couldn't leave the laundry running and go back to the apartment because when she went back, it was likely that someone would have stolen items or pulled the laundry out and dumped it onto the dirty floor.

Soon, the wait became too long and the laundry room too much to handle, Mom started taking her laundry to Nanny's house. For me, it was an adventure. Mom collected laundry into garbage bags, put me in my snowsuit, and piled me and the bags into a small wooden sleigh she could pull down the still snowy sidewalks to her parent's house. Mom had a car sitting in the parking lot, but it didn't run, and there was no money for repairs, so we walked or took the bus everywhere.

Nanny's house was a relatively short walk, laundry was free, and we often stayed for dinner. It was a chance to get a hearty meal with well-done meat, vegetables, and potatoes, plus glass after glass of milk. Nanny was from an era where meat was *always* cooked to well done. Dessert was often cookies from the jar at the end of the breakfast bar. Sometimes I got ice cream. Mom's rule was I couldn't have any if I didn't finish my meal.

"Go on. The ice cream doesn't take up any space. It just slides in between," Nanny said, even if I hadn't eaten all my meal. Usually, my mom gave in, and I got my ice cream.

We were eventually offered an apartment in subsidized housing. In Ottawa, one could be put on a list and wait for a rental unit where the cost was twenty-five percent of your income, no matter what you earned. It was apartment 312, a two-bedroom on the third floor. Sitting in my new bedroom, I could hear the kids from the daycare downstairs playing outside in the fenced-in yard, singing songs and laughing while I was just above them, alone. I pulled my tiny chair over to the window and peered out, trying to get a peek at all the kids, wishing I could play. Instead, my stuffed animals and dolls were my friends, and I served their meals on little plastic plates and fed the baby dolls with tiny plastic spoons. We drank tea and had a picnic on a blanket.

One spring day, after a long winter inside, it was finally warm enough to once again have picnics with my bears and dolls on the balcony. All set up, with blankets laid out, suddenly something came spraying over the edge of the balcony from above. My mom ran out only to discover that a dog had peed over the edge, and it had come down on my stuffed animals, toys, and blankets. She marched upstairs, knocking on the door.

"Excuse me, but I believe your dog just urinated over the balcony edge. Do you realize that it sprays down on the people below you? My daughter was playing, and all her stuffed toys are covered," she said, trying to sound polite.

"Yeah, so what," the woman replied.

"I'm going to need to wash everything and would like you to cover the cost for laundry," Mom said.

"Nah," the woman replied, "I don't think so," and closed the door. My mom stood stunned, and the woman didn't care in the slightest.

"Can you at least keep your dog from peeing off the balcony?" mom shouted through the door, but she never got a reply.

Teddy bears and blankets were put in garbage bags, ready to be brought to the laundry. There were at least two loads, and we didn't have money to spare. The picnics on the balcony stopped after that. We couldn't afford the extra laundry costs, not to mention it was disgusting.

During this time, my mom worked at the post office, and

I spent nights with my grandfather. She would drop off Nanny and pick me up in the morning, and then we'd go back to our apartment. I played in the morning and watched television until just after lunch, when I would take a bus to school. Eating a simple peanut butter sandwich and watching the *Flintstones* on television was the daily routine before heading off for kindergarten. Mom could then sleep for a few hours or try to run errands before I got home. I was to get off the bus, come in the apartment building's main entrance, ring the buzzer, and come upstairs. If my mom wasn't home, I would just wait until someone went in and follow them through the door.

One winter day, she was out, so I sat in the hall outside our apartment, still wearing my snowsuit. The carpet was musty and old, and there was a faint smell of cigarette smoke from the nearby stairwell where people would go to smoke. The hall had little circulation, and the air felt stagnant as the smells lingered. I noticed my damp, cold snowsuit was now warm and wet. I had wet myself while sitting waiting, not even aware it had happened at first. This wasn't the kind of community where I would go to a neighbour and ask to use their bathroom or ask for help. We weren't friendly with our neighbours and kept to ourselves. I had a sense that it could be dangerous. I didn't tell my mom when she got home, fearing her anger. Maybe she didn't notice or was too tired, but that day there were no angry outbursts.

I only had a couple of friends in the neighbourhood—a twin brother and sister who lived in one of the townhouses built around the apartment building. Back then, we called these "the projects." Sometimes when we got off the school bus, I played out in front of the building before heading up to the apartment. One day, the snow had been falling for hours when we got off the bus.

We climbed a large hill left by the snow ploughs, dug out tunnels, and threw snowballs. As I knelt down, I felt a little pain. It turns out that it was from a broken beer bottle thrown into the snow. The brown piece of glass was covered with blood, and the white snow was stained red. It had cut through my snow pants and into my knee.

My friends brought me to their house, which was very close by. Their mother came to the door with a cigarette in her mouth and glared at me.

"Why did you bring her here?" she asked. There was no concern, no comforting words, just anger that I was there. I didn't understand why their mom was mad. I walked home alone and up to the apartment where my mom cleaned the wound and took me to the hospital, just in case I needed stitches. I was lucky but did get a nice scar to remember the event.

My mom suffered from migraines, and at times, they were so terrible she couldn't leave the apartment. One day, she realized we were out of milk and bread, but she couldn't go shopping. She got out a piece of paper and prepared a grocery list. Since I was too young to read, she drew pictures to help me figure out what she wanted me to buy and included the prices and the total for bread, milk, and a few other small items. Mom counted out her nickels, dimes, and quarters to pay for the items. She said if I had to, I could ask the man at the store for help, but it seemed to me that I was supposed to do this on my own. I put on my jacket and shoes and walked down the stairs at the side of the building. The small convenience store was across a small side street right beside the building.

As I opened the door to the store, a small bell rang, announcing my presence to the man behind the counter. I walked straight to the back of the store and picked up the milk, but our normal bread wasn't there when I got to the shelf. I took a moment and picked a different brand, hoping it would be good enough. When I walked up to pay, I could hardly reach the counter. The man leaned over the counter and seemed a little confused. I put my list on the counter without saying a word and started pulling out the change from my jacket pocket. He looked at the list, back at me, and rang through the order. It didn't seem strange to me at the time, but now I realize it was unusual to see a four-year-old shopping alone, even in the projects.

A few weeks later, my friend was eating sour cream and onion chips on the bus home from school. She was so excited because there was a contest, and she had won a free bag. She asked me to go to the store with her to collect her winnings. This was the same store I had been to a few weeks before, and so I agreed. We opened the heavy glass door and walked straight to the chip stand. Row after row of chips of varying flavours stood high above us. For some reason, the cashier at the front of the store didn't notice two small children alone. Outside, we quickly ate the second bag and won another. We were thrilled and proceeded to eat our way through yet another bag of chips. Meanwhile, my mom began to worry that I wasn't home. She called the school, and no one knew where I was until I walked into the apartment forty-five minutes later.

"Where have you been?" she yelled as I opened the door.

"Jeannie won chips, and we went to the store to get a bag, but then she won another bag, so we had to go back," I said proudly.

"I called the school, and I almost called the police. You are to come straight home after school," she said. I had no idea what

I had done wrong, but I was sent to the corner to sit in my small chair to think about what I had done.

Sitting in my small chair in the corner wasn't so bad. I was used to it and could lean my head against the wall and go to sleep. The alternative was a spanking, which I was not fond of. It was the mid-seventies and all the kids I knew got spankings. Television moms would say, "Wait until your father gets home," with the threat of Dad taking out the belt and spanking the child. In our family, Mom had to take on the role of disciplinarian. I, however, was not an easy child to spank. I would sit down on the floor and kick and flail my arms so that my mom couldn't get close to me, and I would scream at the top of my lungs. Sometimes she would win, but often enough, I would hold out until she gave up and sent me to the corner. I sat on the tiny painted wood and wicker chair I'd had since I was a baby. It felt like I got in trouble all the time. I would get in trouble for lying or for not tidying my toys. Often, I wasn't really sure what I was in trouble for, but I sure spent a long time on that chair trying to figure it out or napping.

Toys were not to be left out in our tiny apartment. I was allowed to take out one toy and play with it but had to put it away before taking out others. When I watched *Toy Story* for the first time, many years later, I was perplexed at how Andy, the main character, had different toys out and played with them together. When I played with Mr. Potato Head, I had to put all the pieces away before getting another toy. They didn't mingle together. It wasn't allowed, at least not in my world. Craft supplies were also something used in a very particular manner. I would save them because once they were used, they'd be all gone, and I didn't know when I might get more. Things were meant to be savoured and cherished, not wasted frivolously. This, of course, meant that

I was somewhat restrained in how I played and how often I did crafts. There was no abundance in our life.

There are moments I remember fondly. Sundays were bath nights. We would have dinner, sometimes at my grandparents' house, and I would have a bath while my mom cleaned up and watched 60 Minutes. If I heard the Andy Rooney segment that ended the show, I knew I had to hurry and finish my bath so I could watch the *Wonderful World of Disney*. I was mesmerized by the stories that always seemed to have happy endings. I believed in happy endings.

Mom had started to date a man named Bert. He had a small bachelor apartment that we visited at least once, although all I really remember is that I had to sit in the bathroom and colour while the adults talked in the other room, the only other room in this small bachelor apartment. I guess this is why Bert usually came to our place. During one of Bert's sleepovers, my mom went for a shower, and I was watching cartoons on television, still in my pyjamas. Bert came out of the bedroom in nothing but his underwear and asked me if I wanted to play. He got down on the floor beside me in front of the television and lifted me up to play airplane. He then suggested another game called rub-a-dub-dub. He sat me on top of him and rubbed me back and forth on his now exposed genitals. There was a burning sensation from the friction, and I didn't like it. As soon as he was done, I went back to my cartoons, and he went to the bedroom and dressed. My mom never knew anything had happened. I didn't know anything had happened. It was just a game.

Was it really any different than the games I played with my grandfather?

A few months later, mom asked, "Did you take money

from my purse?" She was missing a few twenty-dollar bills, and that was a lot of money for us back then.

"No," I replied. I had no idea what she was talking about.

"You must have taken it. It was in my purse, and now it's gone. What did you do with it?" She persisted and kept asking if I had taken it. "Did you take it?"

"No," I said again and again. Mom wouldn't stop asking. "Fine. Yes, I took it," I eventually said, figuring it would be easier because then she would stop asking. I'm not sure what went through her mind, but before I knew it, she called the police. I'm not sure what they were supposed to do with a four-year-old, but they came to our apartment. There was a male and female officer in their uniforms, and they stood tall over me. I was scared. I knew I couldn't change my story, but they kept asking questions like what I had done with the money. I hadn't yet perfected the art of lying.

"I threw it in the garbage," I said, thinking if the money was gone, this would be all over.

"Which garbage?" they asked, looking to one another.

"The one near my bus stop" was all I could think of. I don't think they believed me, but they left, and nothing else happened. This was my first terrifying exposure to police. I had lied and thought I was going to be in big trouble. Years later, when I told my mom I wasn't the one who stole the money, she figured that it must have been Bert. She said he gambled and was a bookie. Looking back, that makes far more sense.

Mom didn't have much money for groceries and bills, let alone anything else. She was feeding me but would skip meals herself. She lost a lot of weight, and even though she had always been petite and just over five feet tall, she was down to eighty-seven pounds, looking very frail, from not having enough to eat. There were not many food banks or resources, and in our family, no one asked for help, though my grandparents would have likely brought over groceries. Still, she would never ask, even when they had been bringing groceries to her younger sister. Mom sometimes made spaghetti with meat sauce, one of her specialties, which was inexpensive and made enough for leftovers. The smell was glorious. Once, I took my plate, piled with glorious pasta and sauce to the table. Our apartment was small, and it was only a few steps from the stove to the table, but the pasta was slippery on the plate and slid right off. My mom flipped out. She was angry.

"Why can't you be more careful?" she yelled. I ended up back in the corner. Apparently, I couldn't do anything right. She was barely surviving, and when you aren't sure where your next meal will come from, sometimes your reactions are a little over the top. I know that now, but then, I didn't get it.

In a rare occurrence, Dad called and asked if I could come out to Edmonton to visit. His new wife had a sister in Ottawa who would accompany me on the plane. My mom considered it, although she was still worried. She didn't know this new wife or the woman who would accompany me, and my father was the man who hit her and pushed her down sets of stairs. Despite this, I bounced off the walls at even the remote prospect of seeing my dad.

"How would you like to live in a house with a pool?" he asked me on our next call.

"I'd love that," I said gleefully. To a four-year-old, that would have been better than winning the lottery. A couple of days later, Ethel, or "Ga," as we called her, told my mom not to send me because my dad intended to keep me there. Ethel warned Mom that it would be tough to get me back, and the costs for travelling to Alberta and for lawyers would be more than she could afford. My mom decided to heed the warning. Ethel likely changed the course of my life with that one call. She later shared with my mom that Norman had also been abusive and that it was probably where my dad learned his behaviour. As I would later learn when training to be a psychotherapist, when someone grows up in a home with abuse, the cycle of abuse can pass down through the generations.

Life was weighing hard on Mom, and at times, it became too much for her. A few times when I was acting up, she would say, "If you are so unhappy, I can call Child Services, and they'll come and pick you up." I imagined her packing my little grey suitcase and me standing on the corner outside our apartment building, waiting for a bus to come to pick me up and take me away. Sometimes I wished she would make the call because maybe she would be happier if I wasn't there. I just wanted her to be happy. Mom could be so nice when she was happy.

Despite the tight budget, Mom seemed happy around Christmas and always tried to make it special. She would buy lots of presents. Even if they weren't big gifts, she made sure I had things under the tree to unwrap on Christmas morning. I never realized that we were poor. Even the word "poor" sounds odd to me now. No one ever told me. This was just the way things were.

One Christmas morning, I woke up early and realized I hadn't gotten a gift for my mom. I was devastated. She wouldn't have anything to open. I searched my room for something appropriate. There were a few toys I considered, but I didn't want to give those toys up. I felt a little guilty, but then I saw my globe.

It was about the size of a basketball and was something that an adult might like. I went to the storage room across the hall from my bedroom that my mom used as an office. Her desk barely fit, but it gave her a place to keep stationery and other office supplies.

I pulled out some white writing paper and clear tape and brought it back to my room. I tried in vain to wrap the papers around the sphere, taping each piece to the globe. I brought it out and put it under the tree anyway. It was still a gift Mom could open, even if the wrapping wasn't very good. When she got up, I opened my gifts from Santa and from Mom. I was so happy. Then it was her turn. Mom pulled the paper off the globe, but I don't think she understood it was a gift. She didn't say anything, and she didn't seem as happy with her present as I was with mine. She placed the globe back in my room. My gift hadn't been good enough. Again, the message was that no matter what I did or how hard I tried, nothing I did seemed good enough.

The two years in this apartment were probably the hardest for my mom. She was also dealing with her migraine headaches that got worse and worse. Some days would be so bad she would go to the emergency room, where they would give her a strong painkiller, and she would sleep for a few hours before she was sent home. She saw specialists and tried experimental drugs. One doctor said it might be a brain tumour and suggested she start making arrangements because she might be dead within a couple of years. Mom took this to heart and paid for her funeral and burial plot on a payment plan.

She was barely twenty-six years old. I think the pressure became too much to bear, and one day, she took me to my aunt's apartment. Mom went down to the beach, where she attempted to commit suicide. I didn't know this at the time, and I've never heard the details, but I believe it was an overdose from what I have pieced together. Somehow, she was found and taken to the hospital. They subsequently admitted her to the psychiatric ward for six weeks. My aunt and grandparents took care of me during this time. Mom tells me that no one visited her, and she felt abandoned by her family. It was the seventies and people didn't talk about mental health, especially suicide. I learned of her suicide attempt when I was a teenager. It made me wonder why she would want to leave me and why I wasn't enough. Never feeling like I was enough became a theme for me in years to come.

If there was one person whose approval made me feel good about myself, it was my grandmother, Nanny. Nanny always said she wouldn't babysit any of her grandchildren. She had cared for her own kids and was done with the caregiver role. I do remember being with her when Mom wasn't around. Nanny would sit on the couch, with one foot on the coffee table, and knit. She could knit a sweater in an evening and taught me the craft when I was five. I knitted a scarf for my doll, and by the time I got up the following day, she had knitted a dress, hat, and jacket complete with white angora trim to match the scarf. From that day forward, we could not leave the house until my doll had her jacket and hat on to keep her warm. While Nanny was knitting, I would pretend to be a doctor and wrap her toes in tissue to bandage them up. I was the only one of her grandchildren who spent much time in her home outside of the holidays.

Nanny was a strong-willed woman who just plugged through life. She didn't sugarcoat things and said it like it was. This meant that when she was impressed, it meant something special. It was the gold star of approval to meet Nanny's expectations. She had worked multiple jobs to keep her family fed, and she was never too good to accept any job that presented itself. Nanny had been set to go to university at the age of thirteen, but then World War II started, and that was over. She could do difficult math problems in her head and read an entire novel over her morning toast and tea. This strong and smart woman married and came to Canada, leaving behind any dreams of greater things to make a life for herself and her family.

If there was a standard for hard work, I think Nanny embodied it. To this day, I am persistent because Nanny wouldn't have stopped and given up. She just kept going, no matter what.

chapter 3

About two months after I started grade one, we finally left the confines of apartment living and moved into a townhouse in a new project that seemed like a friendly community. We had been on a waiting list for a townhome and finally, one became available. We lived on one edge of the project with a park and community centre across the street from our front door. There was a wading pool, tennis courts, a baseball diamond, and perfect climbing trees. A wood fortress play structure had recently been built, and from my six-year-old eyes, it seemed to extend into the sky. When winter came, the city built an ice rink, and I strapped on my skates and walked across the street to skate under the single light that stood in the middle of the park.

My bedroom was at the back of the house and looked over our little backyard and the rest of the townhouses beyond. The project was a series of courtyards interspersed with parking lots, all connected by small, paved paths cracked and littered with gum wrappers and cigarette butts. The small lawns had the grass worn down to the dirt from the masses of children playing tag, skipping, shooting marbles, and acting out imaginary games. Within the community, there was a retired old French couple, a British mom with her two daughters, one who was in my class at school, and an Irish single dad with his two very sweet teenage daughters. When the community centre organized a camping trip for some of the kids, those sweet teenage girls saw I didn't have any friends and took me under their wing, sharing their tent with me.

Our two-bedroom townhouse had a master bedroom and second bedroom that two children could easily share, with its two separate closets. I got the whole room and both closets all to myself. One closet had all our family photo albums lined up along the floor with a wood board across the top to make a second shelf where I could put more books. The cupboard held clothes I wore less often, like the pretty dresses Nanny would buy me so I would look nice on picture day at school. The top shelf held board games that weren't played often, as most were four-player games intended for the nuclear family, but not our small two-person home. In the other closet, along the bottom, there was a small ledge beneath the hanging clothes, and there I created a reading and writing nook. I loved sitting in there, hidden away from the world, lost in a book. Mom got some old carpet from Nanny and used it to carpet as much of my room as she could. The first carpet was a hideous brown and yellow, but it was warmer on the feet than the cold cracked tile underneath. Nanny liked to redecorate often, and we were the recipients of many items over the years. Sometimes I think Nanny would redecorate just as an excuse to give us newer furniture.

When we first moved in, there were no appliances, and we had to put our milk and other cold food between the back door and screen door to keep it cold during the chilly fall days. Mom took the time to set up the house. She wallpapered most every wall and hung pictures in every open spot. It was like she was covering every inch of the house around her so she could only see the home she created. We eventually bought a refrigerator and stove, followed soon after by a washer and dryer. No more dingy, dirty laundry rooms for us. By Christmas, we were settled in and happy in our little home.

The neighbour next door was around Mom's age and had a son a little older than me and a daughter who was a little younger. The daughter, Julie, and I would play at the park together and have sleepovers. I was a bit of a homebody, but Mom would encourage me to go outside to play with Julie. I sometimes treated Julie like an annoying younger sister who always wanted to hang out with me.

Once the weather warmed, we would barbecue in the backyard and chat with neighbours. Being outside was a welcome reprieve from the stifling heat in the house. With no air conditioning, Mom would balance a large square fan in her bedroom window to provide a little air circulation, blowing some of the cooler night air into the house. When lying in bed, even with the blankets pushed down, my nightgown would be damp with sweat. With my window open, I could hear the neighbourhood comedies and tragedies play out—people laughing late into the night, getting louder presumably with the more they drank, or sirens coming as another woman was beaten by her husband. My grandfather would call, updating us on the police activity on our street. He often listened to the police channel on that same shortwave radio that I played with a couple of years before.

Mom and I became friends with some of the more colourful locals and would spend evenings in the courtyard, sitting on old aluminum webbed lawn chairs and front steps. The adults would drink beer, and the kids would roam the neighbourhood, all together in groups of ten or twenty, just after dusk. A favourite game was Ghost in the Graveyard. Some nights the games ran late, and the stories shared by the adults got more colourful. One woman had a man living with her and her three kids. He took off his shirt one night to show us the bullet hole wound on his chest where he had been shot. He then turned to expose his scarred back where the bullet exited and tore apart half his back. He chuckled as the kids gasped.

A couple of houses down from ours, there was a short man named George, with curly black hair and a potbelly. His rusted red and white tow truck was parked behind his dirt bare backyard where some of the neighbourhood guys would hang out and do odd jobs for him, fixing cars to make a little pocket money. There never seemed to be much work for them, as more often than not, they sat drinking beer, while George's dogs swarmed around the yard. When I was eight, George asked me to work for him, taking messages for his home business. I was also responsible for keeping the dogs quiet and letting them outside periodically. George would take in the odd stray dog. He ended up with fifteen dogs when two females had a litter of pups two weeks apart. The guys who worked for George were like odd strays he took in to help. One of those neighbourhood strays, Adam, had dirty blonde hair and always seemed to have day-old stubble on his dark tanned face that was deeply wrinkled and pitted, even though he wasn't that old. He liked to come over and talk to my mom. It was fun at first as his nieces and nephew lived in the courtyard, and we would all play together. I slept at their house a couple times and finally started building up a larger friend group.

Adam would come over to our house to have a beer and hang out. My mom was polite, maybe too polite, and he didn't seem to take a hint when it was time to go. At first, he seemed nice enough, but soon, he stopped by all the time. Mom couldn't go out the back door to her car without him coming over to talk to her. She finally made it clear that she wasn't interested in him as anything beyond a friend. He got mad and stormed off, but he returned the next day.

"Let me in. Can we talk?" he said, knocking on the door.

"Adam, there's nothing to talk about. Please go home," Mom replied.

"Just let me in," he said more loudly, banging on the screen door, the metal frame rattling.

"Please leave," she said, almost pleading. He kept banging, but she ignored it. She told me to go up to my room. I could hear the banging and was scared.

What was he doing? Why was he so mad?

Then it stopped, and a sense of relief washed over me. He was gone. A few minutes later, I heard the back gate squeak, followed by loud banging on the back door.

"Let me in, you bitch," he yelled. Then I heard the shattering of glass. He had banged the window of the screen door so hard it shattered. Through my window, I saw him head across the parking lot into the maze of townhouse courtyards. Mom was scared and called the police, who arrived half an hour later. They asked a few questions and left.

Mom swept up the broken glass, and the next day, Grandpa brought over an old screen door and installed it for us. After this, whenever Mom would go to her car, she would check out the window first to see if Adam was around. He would be sitting in George's backyard, a couple of houses down, glaring at her.

"Don't look at him. Walk straight to the car," she said to me as we would be leaving.

A few weeks passed with menacing glares from him, but otherwise, things were quiet. One Friday night, we could hear the usual neighbourhood partying and drinking through the open windows. Music was playing, and voices got louder outside. Then, there was a rap on the door.

"I know you're in there. Let me in. I just wanna talk," he said. Usually, people leave their main door open to let the breeze through on warm summer nights. We had taken to keeping our door closed most of the time, but this hot evening the door was open. He banged louder.

"I have nothing to say to you. Please just go away," she said as she walked over to the door. He pulled on the screen door, and despite it being locked, the latch gave way, and he pushed his way into the house. I was in the living room in the corner, huddled on the couch, afraid to move. Mom was blocking him from coming in, yelling at him to get out of our house. In anger, he smashed his fists down on our stereo. The plastic cover on the turntable shattered and crushed. Mom called the police, and Adam ran off. They arrived and took a report and left again, but it seemed like nothing would be done.

Adam started waiting outside our house and following my mom. He was stalking her, although stalking wasn't something heard about back then. Mom got a restraining order and would call the police anytime he was around, but he would disappear. She lived in fear of what he would do next, not knowing if the police would arrive fast enough or if he would again break into our house. Somehow, this all felt normal. The police were at some of our neighbours' homes often enough. I later learned that the guy with the bullet wound was part of a motorcycle gang, and the house where I had slept over was used for drug dealing. Another neighbour was charged with the attempted murder of her husband. When a police officer was shot in a nearby shopping mall, the SWAT team stormed our neighbourhood, and the shooter was found in a house at the far end of our parking lot. I watched the whole scene unfold from my bedroom window. This was all normal in the projects, so why wouldn't it spill over into my own house? It was just the way things were.

Soon, I was no longer allowed to hang out with the kids in the courtyard. There were no more games at dusk or sleepovers. I played in the house more often and isolated myself from most of the neighbours. Julie, the girl next door, was the only person I would hang out with. We grew closer, even though we sometimes squabbled like siblings. I was mean to her and treated her like an annoying younger sister, but we remained friends somehow into our teen years. She was the one and only friend from the old neighbourhood who I remember with fondness. I wish I had been a better friend to her.

chapter 4

Mom had stopped working night shifts, and the sleepovers with my grandfather ended. He did, however, continue to play a huge role in my life. Mom's car was once again not working and too expensive to fix. So, every Saturday morning, my grandparents would drive to our house and pick us up at exactly 9:30 a.m. to buy groceries. I could set my watch by their arrival. We had to be ready to go, shoes and jacket on, waiting. The car would arrive, and we would bolt out of the house for the short ride to the store.

Once at the grocery store, Nanny would let me ride in her shopping cart, and her first stop was always the bakery where she would buy a half dozen chocolate-dipped donuts. She would open the box and give me one to eat while we finished shopping. As I got older, I was too big to sit in the cart, but I would still follow her around the store and eat my Saturday chocolate donut. Grandpa would walk around on his own and make bird calls as he shopped. He would smile to himself as he saw people look around, wondering where the birds were. He talked to all the store staff. Some laughed and smiled while others peered at him strangely, a little uncertain.

"Stop flirting with the girls, Bill," Nanny would say to him with a stern look. After the shopping was done, we would stop at my grandparents' house for lunch. There was nothing quite like freshly sliced ham from the deli on thick slices of still-warm bread from the bakery. Just a little butter and the perfect sandwich was made. No toppings were needed. After lunch, Grandpa would drive us home, and this was when he started giving me an allowance. My mom would be carting brown paper grocery bags to the house, and as I climbed out from the back seat of the car, he would slip a twenty-dollar bill into my hand.

"Don't tell your mother," he smiled. This ritual continued every time I went anywhere with him and was another secret I had to keep.

Grandpa also started taking me to the library every three weeks. He would arrive in the evening after dinner, and we would drive to the local public library. I loved books, so this was a wondrous place where I could borrow books on any topic that I could imagine. We headed back after the three-week borrowing timeframe was up, and I would return the previous selections and get new ones. I found *Lassie Come Home*, the biggest book I had borrowed up until that time. It was a hardcover novel, and the library had three identical copies. I didn't want anyone to know that I hadn't been able to read the whole book in the allotted time frame. I was self-conscious about my reading skills even though I was only eight years old. I would take note of the page number I had read to, walk up to the counter and return the book. I would then go into the children's section. At the same time, my grandfather examined the adult section in another room. I would scurry to the bookshelf to get one of the other copies of *Lassie Come Home*, always worried that they might not be available. I did this exchange ritual at least three or four times before I managed to get through it. No one could know I was a slow reader. That would be mortifying.

Sometimes, Grandpa would take the scenic route home. He would drive around or stop in a parking lot at the local nature trails that were only a few minutes away from the library.

"I have something to show you," he said as he reached under the seat in his car and pulled out adult magazines. He had to put the magazine into my hands as I wouldn't take it. I knew they were dirty magazines and not for kids. He opened it and thumbed through the pages stopping at certain spots.

"What do you think of this?" he asked. There were pictures of naked women, and I didn't know what to think. It was uncomfortable looking at them, but I didn't say anything. When he was satisfied, he took the magazines and put them back under the seat. The next time we went to the library, he insisted I take one of the magazines home with me, so I put it in my canvas bag along with the library books. He slipped a twenty-dollar bill into my hand as I got out of the car, and I walked up to my house with my library books and new magazine hidden in my canvas school bag. I took that magazine straight to my room and hid it behind the books in my closet.

Eventually, several magazines accumulated in their hiding spot, and I would have this dread hang over me that my mom might find them one day. If I came home from school and she had cleaned my room, I would panic, thinking she might find them. I learned how to hide things well.

I wanted to tell her, but it always played out the same way. Mom would come to my room and sit on my bed, likely noticing there was something wrong.

"What's up?" she asked.

"I don't know."

"Is there something you want to tell me?" she asked, followed by silence, as she gave me the space to say whatever was on my mind. I dared not to make eye contact, worrying she could see my thoughts. The words I wanted to say welled up in my mind, wanting to pour out, but something held them back. I couldn't tell her about the magazines. It would ruin everything. Mom might be mad at Grandpa. Then everyone would know I was looking at dirty pictures, and everything might change. I maintained my silence.

Mom had dated a few guys on and off, but around the time I was nine years old, she started dating Chris. He had black hair with a receding hairline, a beard, and dark eyes. He had a dark green car that meant fewer Saturday shopping trips with my grandparents, but he wasn't much of a presence to me beyond that.

My mom seemed happier, and we had more people around. Some parties filled our tiny townhouse with friends and neighbours, and it was fun to hang out with all the adults, some who would give me drinks like punch spiked with rum and "chocolate milk" that was actually Kahlua and milk. Chris made friends in the neighbourhood, and we started to feel like part of the community again, despite past events with Adam. Chris eventually moved in with us and was a regular fixture. With a little more money to go around, we were to be able to do things like go to the drive-in and buy new things, like our very first computer, the Vic 20. This was a big deal because many kids at school didn't have one yet. Mostly, we played video games, but I taught myself some basic programming from library books. There were hundreds of code lines to type in, without mistakes, to create a single, simple video game. I was growing up in the height of the eighties, listening to Madonna on a cassette in my ghetto blaster, pinning posters of Tom Cruise, Bon Jovi, and Bruce Springsteen on my bedroom wall, and going to the local arcade to watch the boys play video games for hours on a single quarter.

    Mom and I started going to Chris's family celebrations, and his nieces became quick friends of ours. His family was like a second family to me, unlike my dad's family, whom I only saw maybe once a year. Christmas was split between time with Chris's family and ours. He had a daughter from his previous marriage that was a couple of years younger than I, and she would sometimes spend weekends with us. We spent time with Chris' sister and nieces and nephew often and they too became friends. Chris was also close with his mother. She was a former schoolteacher, very proper in her white blouses, smart pants, and dyed blonde hair, always perfectly coiffed. The kids all called her Momma Bea because her granddaughter was also Bea.

    We enjoyed driving out to the country in Chris' car and visited a place my mom called the Old Mansion. She had been bringing me there since I was quite young. We would pick apples and wildflowers to bring home. The Old Mansion remained as ruins from an estate home that had stood fully furnished when my mom was a teenager. After a fire destroyed the wood frame, all that was left were the stone walls. Mom became more adventurous with Chris, and we sometimes visited this place late in the evening. The crickets would chirp, and the stars above would shine brightly, far from the city lights. We even did a few of these excursions in the winter, trudging in snowsuits through deep snow in the dark. It was a magical place to go as a kid.

    Time passed, but the months with Chris became peppered with more and more fights. I would go to bed, my stuffed animals all lined up, tucked in on each side of me, wondering if tonight there'd be another fight. Blue Bear, my favourite, was always right beside me. He had a music box inside that wound up with a key on his back and played Brahms' lullaby. I would wind up the bear and place it right up to my ear to block out the sound of them yelling. It didn't work, and I could still hear them, but it gave me something else to focus on. When the arguments lasted longer or got louder than normal, I would cry myself to sleep, curled up listening to my bear's music box, over and over again.

One evening, the fight made its way upstairs, and my mom came into my room. Chris came bursting through the door after her and shoved her backward. She fell next to my bed and hit her jaw on my tiny wooden and wicker chair, the same one I used to sit on when I was put in the corner for being bad. Her jaw quickly swelled, and she made her way to the hospital, where they were sure it was broken. She was lucky that time. It wasn't broken, although she would suffer from jaw pain for the rest of her life. After these fights, she kicked Chris out, and the house would be quiet and peaceful again. I loved it when he was gone because Mom was much nicer. She played with me and seemed a little kinder. We would go on drives out to the country, just the two of us. She would point out the flowers and plants that grew wild, and we would enjoy a picnic lunch in the sun. But inevitably, she would let Chris come back.

Mom's migraines were frequent, with several trips to the hospital and more and more days spent in bed. I don't remember my exact age (probably around ten or eleven), but I do remember the night in great detail. Chris and I were watching television while mom slept upstairs, suffering through yet another migraine. There were only a couple of movie channels back then, and this evening, there was a cartoon movie with Betty Boop. We sat on the couch in the tiny living room, and Chris put his arm around me. He looked down at me and kissed me ever so gently. This was how I had imagined the boy I had a crush on might one day kiss me.

Chris paused, measuring my response, then he kissed me more deeply. I liked the attention. He continued kissing me, and his hands ran over my body through my clothes. This was wrong, but I was sure I had done something to suggest I wanted it.

Had I flirted with him?

He took my hand and pushed it down on his tight jeans. He was bulging and then undid his zipper. He then moved my hand back and forth. He laid himself behind me and pulled off my underwear. He began to push himself into me, but it hurt. I was facing the television, and my eyes fixated on Betty Boop. The song she sang rang through my ears, over and over. He tried for a while from the front and back, rubbing himself on me, but did not penetrate me. I was too small. He turned me around and guided my head down. He forced himself into my mouth and pushed my head up and down until he came. My mouth filled, and I thought I was going to choke. He gave me a soda, and it was over. We went back to watching television as if nothing had happened. I went to bed, ashamed.

The next time it happened was months later. It was summer, and Mom worked cleaning houses while I was home for summer vacation. He brought me to their queen-size waterbed and laid me down. It was more of the same with minimal penetration but plenty of painful friction. He was interrupted when the doorbell rang. He got up, pulled on his jeans, and went to answer the door but then came back upstairs to finish what he started. There was at least one more time when again, Mom was sick, and he took me down to the basement. The basement was unfinished, with exposed concrete floors and wood studs on the walls, but Mom had it set up as a play area where I would play with my Barbies. There was an old double bed, a sort of guest room, for anyone who might want to stay over. Chris undressed me from the waist down. First, he pushed himself into my mouth and then climbed on top of me. I hadn't got my period yet but wondered if I could be pregnant and how would I ever know. In health class, I was told I could get pregnant before my first period. My only other sex ed was what my grandfather showed me in the adult magazines during our ongoing trips to the library.

In winter, my grandfather added trips to the nature trails where we could feed the chickadees. If I stood still enough with seed on an open palm, the birds would come down and land on my hand to eat. The magazines would be brought out at the end of these hikes and were more and more explicit. They included men and women together. My grandfather cut out a man's photo with an erect penis and another of a naked woman, legs spread wide. He had mounted the pictures on construction paper like some school art project, cut a slit in the woman, and showed me how the penis would enter. He said he wanted me to understand sex. It was like some sick paper dolls.

When summer came, he would take me out in his canoe to the middle of the river, far from anyone. He was very careful about where we went, never to the beach or boat launches. We went to the bird sanctuary, and he would drag the canoe through the mud out onto the river, away from prying eyes. He always brought his vintage, khaki green messenger bag from his Air Force days with a couple of cans of pop and maybe a few snacks. He brought bathing suits for me to wear, tiny string bikinis, some made of sheer fabric that could be seen through. There was a small sandbar hidden amongst the reeds, and I would have to model the bikinis so he could take photos. We would dive off the canoe and swim in the cool fresh water on those hot summer days out on the river. As we swam, he would pull me close and kiss me deeply, the roughness of the stubble on his cheek prickling my face. He would hold me tight to his body.

I started telling my mom that I didn't want to go with Grandpa, even though I loved swimming and canoeing. I wanted to hang out with friends or do homework. Anything to avoid more uncomfortable situations. Mom would argue with me. "You should appreciate everything he does for you," and so I would give in and go out with my grandfather again. One day, instead of magazines, he pulled out a thin cardboard box from under his seat. He told me to open it. Inside was a long plastic object. He explained how to turn it on and how to use it. It was a vibrator. He said that I could use it to prepare myself for when I had sex the first time. The vibrator came home with me and took its place along with the adult magazines, hidden in my closet behind the teen romance and Judy Blume books I collected.

chapter 5

Chris had brought home a small Doberman puppy, and I instantly fell in love. The puppy would run and roll across the carpet in the living room and nuzzle under my chin. Within a week, however, he started to bite. He would run at me and pierce my hand with his razor-sharp baby teeth. My mom tried to train him, but Chris would get him to bite more. He seemed to want the puppy to become aggressive, so I stopped playing with it because I was getting hurt. My mom got mad, Chris yelled, and the puppy was gone. I later learned that Chris took the dog and dropped him on the side of the road somewhere. It was just another fight in a long line of weekly battles in our house.

    I don't know how most of the fights started, just that the voices would get louder, and things would get broken due to the conflicts. Whenever Chris would leave, he would collect his things and usually took the television, VCR, and some other electronics he had brought into the house. The last time he left, he decided to take the new Commodore 64 computer, printer, and modem that I had gotten the previous Christmas. Mom would allow a lot, but she would not let him touch my Christmas presents. As he grabbed our television that was used as a monitor for the computer, she hid the computer, printer, and modem in my bedroom closet while he was taking things to his car. She sat down and waited next to me on my bed, listening for his car to drive off. Then we heard the sound of the back door creaking open and his heavy steps up the stairs. He grabbed a few more things and then headed back down. From the top of the stairs, I watched, and everything was in slow motion. I imagined myself jumping on him, wanting to hit him and hurt him, to push him down the stairs. My mother was beside me and must have sensed something. She put her hand on my shoulder, and the anger drained away. It was over, and he was gone with a slam of the door. The house was quiet once again.

After Chris was kicked out for the final time, I still hadn't gotten my first period. On a trip out with my grandfather, I asked him what happens if a girl gets pregnant and how she would know. He talked about sperm and the mechanics, but I still worried that maybe Chris had gotten me pregnant, and I wouldn't know. I never told him about Chris, and presumably, he thought I was having sex with boys at school because the next time I saw him, he gave me condoms.

A couple of weeks later the police came to our house. Two cops who introduced themselves as Detective Hall and Detective Evans stood at our door. Detective Evans was tall, had broad shoulders, and short brown hair. He wore a sports jacket and looked like the detectives I'd seen on television. Detective Hall was much thinner and had auburn hair with a deeply receding hairline. His most noticeable feature was the many scars on his head. I wondered what kind of police fight had given him so many scars. He had a kind face. They asked to come in and look around. My mom, not knowing anything was wrong, let them in, and they began to search our home. It later came out that Chris had called Crime Stoppers, a local anonymous crime tip line, with a reward for tips that led to an arrest. He told them there was stolen property in our house. My mom had no idea that the items

Chris had purchased, which we thought were used, were, in fact, stolen property.

The detectives started pulling out electronics and asking my mom to prove she had bought them. She was meticulous with her files and started pulling out papers and receipts from a filing cabinet next to her desk in her room. They asked about our stereo, my ghetto blaster, even small things like clock radios. It was ridiculous because no one would have receipts for everything in their house. When she couldn't provide proof for a few of the items Chris had left behind, they arrested her. She asked if she could change from her shorts into jeans, and Detective Hall went upstairs to make sure she didn't try to leave. Detective Evans came to the living room where I sat, looked me straight in the eye, and said, "You're never going to see your mother again. She's going to prison." As my mom came downstairs, she asked the detective if she could call my grandparents so they could take care of me. They allowed the call, and she told me to take my bike and head straight there. The bike ride was short, but the welcome was not warm. My grandparents were upset. I can only imagine what it was like to hear the police arrested your daughter.

The next morning, I biked home early, and mom was back. Her eyes were puffy and red, and she told me about being fingerprinted and having to spend the night in a jail cell. She was charged with five counts of possession of stolen property. A person is guilty with a possession charge until they can prove their innocence, so it is an uphill battle to fight this in court. A couple of days later, the two detectives appeared in the local newspaper with a picture of not only stolen property found in our house but several others too. The article read that they had hit upon a major house break-in ring, and several people were arrested who had been selling stolen property. My mom was mortified that her name appeared in the newspaper. She had never done anything wrong in her life except the one and only parking ticket she got downtown when we went to watch a parade.

Despite her arrest, my life continued much the same. My friends at school were at an age where we started to have class parties. A parent let their child invite the whole class over, and we cleared the furniture in the basement, dimmed the lights, and danced. I was nervous about going to the first party after my mom's arrest. I kept wondering if she was alright. What if she was arrested and taken away again? Halfway through the night, I found a landline in the house, this being before cell phones, and called home to check on her. The tables were turned, and I was the one checking on my mother instead of the other way around. I left the party early because I wanted to take care of her. I think I had been trying to take care of her for a long time. For years, I had hidden the things my grandfather and Chris did because I thought I needed to protect her. Now, I needed to be there to make sure she was alright.

Mom got a lawyer through Legal Aid, but it was nearly a year until the preliminary trial. Her lawyer provided her with a full transcript of the preliminary proceedings so she could make notes that might help him with her case. I sat with the hundred-plus pages and went through them line by line. I made notations in the margins about inaccuracies and questions to follow up. Even though I was only twelve, I started taking out criminal law books on my trips to the library with my grandfather. If I had to go with him, I might as well make good use of the trips. I devoured everything I could find about the law, trials, and evidence. I imagined that somehow, I could make a difference and help Mom get through this.

It was almost another year before the case went to trial, and her lawyer, Mr. Bennett, thought I might be able to testify. To prep me for court, we went to his office that was in a historic house built in the 1800s. The wooden staircase up to his office creaked, and the chunky wood banister was worn from thousands of hands gliding up and down those stairs. The air had a slight musty smell, not of mold or mildew, but aged books. I sat in his office in an oversized leather chair and listened to his questions, answering as best I could. When I was done, he told my mom that it might be helpful to have me testify.

A few days later, we stood in the hallway outside the courtroom, waiting. Mr. Bennett was chatting with my mom, and I watched her look around nervously, worried she would see Chris. I looked up at my mom and then her lawyer.

Should I tell them about Chris and what he had done? Would this be the thing that helped the jury know that he was a bad man, not to be trusted or believed? Could this be the evidence to win her case? No. They won't believe me. They will say I made it up to help my mom. No one will believe me if I say anything now. Why hadn't I said something before?

My mom went into the courtroom with her lawyer, but I had to wait outside on the wood bench until I was called. My aunt waited with me. I worried if I had made the right choice. I was called in and walked up to the stand. As I sat on the chair, the stand came up to my mid-chest. The jurors wouldn't have seen much more than my shoulders and head from the jury box. Mr. Bennett asked me about Chris, the things he brought home, and about him getting home electronics from the company where he worked. It seems that some of the unsold stock of fancy computerized office phones had made their way into our house. I was nervous up on that stand, peering out at a courtroom full of people, seeing my mom sitting in front of me, and wondering if I was messing it all up. The lawyer's questions sounded like they were garbled, and I have no idea if I answered them with any clarity. My mind whirled in fear and confusion. A piece of metal was attached to the stand's underside, and I fidgeted with it while I spoke. Suddenly, it came off into my hands. I was terrified that I would get in trouble if the judge found out I had broken something.

There was no cross-examination. I finished testifying, hid the piece of metal in my hand, and later deposited it into the garbage. Done. Even with all my knowledge and attempted study of the law and transcripts, I felt like I had failed. I went over my answers in my head and decided I had made things worse. In my mind, the fact that the prosecution didn't cross-examine me obviously meant I had helped their case, not my mom's.

Mom was found not guilty on four of the five charges. When Chris left, he had taken our television, and Mom went to one of his friends to buy another TV. She didn't know it was stolen, but since she bought it herself, it seems they had to find her guilty. She was given probation for one year and a stern talking-to from the judge. She has often since repeated a line he spoke that she felt was so very insulting, "When you sleep with the dogs, you are bound to get fleas."

After the trial, I realized there could be no evidence of anything that had happened with Chris or my grandfather. If any of it came out and Mom knew that maybe I could have changed her trial outcome, she would hate me forever and never forgive me. I could never tell her. I had done something wrong, and the shame weighed me down.

The gifts from my grandfather had to go. One afternoon, when she was out, I took the magazines and ripped the pages and covers in strips. Then I tore them into tiny pieces. I put the evidence in the bottom of the garbage bag and was sure there was kitchen waste on top, so Mom would not see the pieces of the magazines. Then I took out the thin cardboard box with the vibrator. It was heavy, and I was scared that mom might notice it in the garbage. I was paranoid about anyone finding it.

What if an animal tore the garbage bag once it was outside for pick up at the end of the week?

I took the vibrator out of the box and placed it on the concrete basement floor. I went over to the orange toolbox, pulled out a hammer, and proceeded to smash the vibrator. It took more force than I expected, but I felt a little lighter with each swing of the hammer. There were shards of off-white plastic and pieces from the motor scattered across the floor. I spread the pieces through the garbage and tore the box into tiny shreds, just like I had seen my mom do with personal documents when she threw them out.

My secret went out with the garbage, and I didn't have to worry about getting caught. I no longer had anything to hide, or so I thought.

PART 2
consequence

chapter 6

With Chris gone, life should have been simpler. There were no more fights between my mom and him, and there was no more abuse. My secrets' weight was lifted with the destruction and disposal of all the so-called gifts from my grandfather. This could have been a significant turning point for me, one that would be scripted in movies with a happy ending where I go on and have a great life. But reality is different. I was wandering on a path, lost and uncertain of where I was headed. I didn't know what I wanted from life, but then I was only a teenager. No one in my family had gone to university. No one at home talked about career paths, and no one shared aspirations for the future. Even though, after years of turmoil, our life was quieter, we were still just existing. I didn't know what I wanted in life because I didn't know what was possible. I had no real dreams for my future.

Are happy endings a real thing? Can I have a normal life? Where do I go from here?

My mom had struggled for so long with migraines that her future was uncertain. She didn't know if she could work a full-time job, so she worked for herself, cleaning people's houses. Mom had dreams of publishing her life story, and in her spare time, in the evenings, she would sit at the desk in her bedroom and pound out page after page of her memoirs on an old manual typewriter. Each page was neatly three-hole punched and placed in a white binder. One day, she let me read the early chapters.

I think she wanted me to understand her life and maybe my own. As I read about my father attempting suicide before they were married and my own mother's suicide attempt when I was around four years old, any fantasies of what my life could have been were crushed. She wrote of being raped and of the strained relationship with her family.

Was a happy life even possible?

We still lived in the projects, but I was isolated from the people who lived around me. I no longer saw a neighbourhood filled with kids playing at the park together. I saw the fights between teenaged boys that left them bloodied and bruised, and I feared the kids from the rival neighbourhood who were known to steal bikes right out of the backyards. I hung out with the girls I went to school with that were from another neighbourhood, and mostly Mom allowed me to do whatever I wanted. My curfew was far later than any of my friends from school. I could go where I wanted and often did. I recall taking the bus downtown, meeting up with a guy I had only met once before. A few times, I ended up at a boy's house, drinking warm beer that we had delivered to the door. It seemed the delivery services weren't too careful checking IDs.

The trips home were interesting as I would hope I was sober enough not to get caught by my mother, and I would use breath mints or gum to mask the smell of beer from my breath. Often Mom wasn't around when I got home, and I could steal away to my room, undetected. There was a day when I brought Julie, the girl next door, with me to go hang out and drink. Unfortunately, her mom was really worried, not knowing where we were, and our moms confronted us when we finally got home. Mom could smell some sort of liqueur on me. Apparently, the mints didn't hide anything but rather made the beer smell like some other alcohol.

    Boys had become the center of my attention, and by junior high my hormones were raging. My friends and I were all exploring the boundaries of these newfound relationships. It seemed that every other week one of my friends was dating a new person or embroiled in some drama with their current boyfriend. There was a sense of freedom that seemed fun, but there was little guidance from my mom. Sex talks or discussions about relationships and respecting yourself were not part of the conversation. I remember only feeling like I should hide things from my mom or else be criticized for doing something wrong. I had learned, oh so well, how to hide things in the past, so I was good at getting away with whatever I wanted. She didn't know what I was going through, so she had no reason to worry about me. The reality was that she didn't know what I was getting into or didn't see it as she began rebuilding her own life.

    I tried smoking as all the cool kids were doing it. Mom would smell the cigarette smoke on me and find the cigarettes in my purse, so I knew I had to figure out how to hide them. I had an old-school calculator that was almost an inch thick. I pulled the calculator apart and took out the board and battery compartment, leaving enough room for a half dozen cigarettes. I could walk around with the calculator in my purse, and Mom never knew. Luckily, I didn't really like smoking, and it was expensive, so I stopped within a few weeks. Looking back, I tend to believe that I do not have an addictive personality—if that is a thing. I could have easily fallen into smoking, drinking, or drugs, but somehow, they never stuck.

    I soon had a new crush, Kyle, who sat next to me in class.

I would go home and pine over him, wishing he would notice me. He was tall, with sandy brown hair, lean muscular build, and when we spoke, the softness in his blue eyes exuded gentleness and kindness. We talked on the phone for hours. Mom hated it and would get mad because with no call waiting in those days, our phone line was always busy, and no one could call her.

When talking with Kyle, he shared fears that he was adopted and told me about the fights he had with his brother. He revealed all his secrets, but I offered very little of myself, content with the bit of attention he gave me.

How could I tell anyone about what had happened to me? I was ashamed that maybe I had done something wrong, and I buried it all deep inside. Chris no longer existed in my world, and I still didn't know that what my grandfather did wasn't normal. Maybe it was just who he was, like the stories people tell about their weird uncle or crazy aunt. My grandfather was weird, and I didn't like what he did, but I didn't know how messed up it was. There was often an internal conflict.

If it is normal, then why are you hiding it? It feels wrong and dirty, but I've let it go on too long now to stop it. What would people think of me? They might think I liked it or wanted it all to happen. Maybe what he did isn't so bad. He never hurt me like Chris. Maybe I am overreacting. If I tell, and it all comes out, what will Nanny think? Will she be mad at me? I can't have that. Maybe there's something wrong with me, and I'm the weird one.

Despite my ongoing internal struggles, life went on. On the outside, I appeared relatively normal. I had friends and partook in school activities. My grandfather had previously bought me skis and boots when I was ten, so when the opportunity to go skiing with the school arose in junior high, I wanted to go. No one seemed to think anything might be wrong with me still using the same boots from three years earlier. Monday nights, a large group would get on a bus straight from school to go skiing until late in the evening. I had grown from the age of ten to thirteen, but I didn't tell my mom the boots were too small because she might not have allowed me to go. It was enough of an expense already. However, it was important for me to go. When I was skiing, I was normal. I was like all my other friends.

I always got in as many runs on the ski hills as I could, stopping only for a few minutes to warm up and quickly eat a small dinner in the chalet. I would stay out on the hill to the last possible minutes before we had to get back on the bus to go home, maximizing my time there. Halfway through the season, I noticed my feet getting cold on a particularly frigid night but ignored it. After a while, I no longer felt the cold and happily kept skiing. As I got on the bus, my toes began to tingle. I pulled off my boots and rubbed my feet, trying to warm them up. I thought nothing of it and chatted with my friends back to the city. When I got home, I took a hot bath as I often did after skiing, then curled up in bed, exhausted from a long day. I was okay until about 4:00 a.m., when I woke up from a dream of flames under my toes. It felt like my toes were on fire. I found a bucket, filled it with cold water, and dipped my toes in to find relief. I was exhausted and drifted in and out of sleep as I sat on the edge of the couch with my feet in the bucket.

When morning came, I told my mom I had been up all night, and my toes were in pain. She didn't believe me, and I should not have been surprised. Why would anything change now? I was once again that four-year-old little girl accused of stealing money that I hadn't taken. I was just this bad kid who was lazy, and my pain was insignificant. She did relent and let me stay home, perhaps because it was easier than putting up a fight. It wasn't until the next day, when my toes were so swollen that I couldn't put on shoes or boots, that she brought me to see our family doctor. He told her that I was lucky I hadn't lost any toes as they were damaged from frostbite.

It was two weeks before I could walk or even get boots on again and go back to school. The skin went black, and a thick layer peeled off. My toes were very sensitive to the cold and still tender to walk on. My grandfather offered to drive me to and from school so I didn't have to take the bus. He always did things like that to keep me in his life, and the truth is I liked the luxury of being driven on the cold winter days. I no longer accepted the magazines but still had to listen to him ask about my sex life, like I had one. Some days, he offered my friends a ride home too, but they soon stopped going with us because they found him creepy. He would arrive early and sit in the school's driveway, not far from my classroom. Some days he walked up to the windows and would peer in. The teacher laughed it off, even though it was awkward and weird, but no one told him to stop.

Within a couple of months, the weather warmed up, and I gladly went back to taking the bus. I was relieved to be away from him. The ongoing strangeness of my relationship with my grandfather and the nonexistent relationship with my father, not to mention the abusive nature of the relationship with Chris, meant I never learned how to love a father figure or even know what that could look like. The internal struggles continued.

Perhaps my relationship with my grandfather is one of convenience and obligation. I tolerate his behaviour but receive things in return, such as an allowance. Damn, that makes me feel disgusting. Am I to blame for what happened? If I didn't put a stop to it, then I must have wanted it to continue so I am in the wrong. How is any of this okay? Why me?

When Grandpa did eventually die, many years later, I did not feel sadness, nor hatred, just indifference.

I built a wall of that indifference around myself. I didn't care about much in my life. Home was just a place to sleep. It was normal for a kid to start to replace their parents with friends as the most important people in their lives, and school was a place where I could be with friends. I went along with whatever they wanted so I could feel like I was part of something. My friends and I had found a small store downtown that sold drug paraphernalia, leather accessories, rock band t-shirts, and buttons with provocative statements. I had covered my jean jacket with buttons that would raise eyebrows from people on the bus as they read them. The buttons said things like, "Let's play post office. You lick, and I'll deliver." Or "Sex is like snow. You never know how many inches you will get or how long it's going to last."

I now wonder why my mom never stopped her thirteen-year-old daughter from wearing these highly inappropriate buttons. It felt like she didn't care what I did. My perceptions of sex were on display for all to see and read, yet no one ever said anything. For my fourteenth birthday, my friends bought me a t-shirt that said, "I only sleep with the best." I was still a virgin, but this was the persona my friends and I wanted to portray. We wanted to be seen as adults, and sex was part of that, even if we weren't actually having sex. We thought it made us look more mature. Mom may have raised an eyebrow but only made a joke asking if the t-shirt referred to my cat who slept with me at night.

I still had a crush on Kyle, but nothing ever happened

between us despite the time spent on the phone and my belief we were getting closer. I still desperately needed validation, so I sought it from other boys. There were parties at friends' houses with a lot of making out in the basement and a little exploration, but it was still innocent.

Kara and Elaine were my closest friends, and we did everything together. Kara was just a little taller than me with sandy brown hair that she had started spiking. She was smart, and school came to her easily. She finished her homework in half the time it took me and earned straight As in everything she did. Elaine was tall and very thin with beautiful dark hair that cascaded down her back with large natural curls. Kara was dating a cute older guy, and they'd already had sex. From my point of view, I was woefully behind and insignificant because a boy hadn't slept with me yet. When Kara's older brother, Patrick, and his friends invited us to go out with them, we jumped at the opportunity. They were two years older than us and good-looking. Patrick had a muscular build from years of karate.

It was a warm spring, and we headed to Kara's house to meet up with the guys. Her mother was standing by the kitchen sink, mixing Jack Daniel's and apple juice in glass bottles and putting them into brown paper lunch bags for Patrick and his friends. It was Apple Jack's, or so I was told. Kara was working, but Patrick had invited us to go along with them anyway. In retrospect, I realized it was all planned out that way. We were paired off with the guys for the evening. Elaine ended up with Greg, and I was with Patrick. The sun was just starting to set across the river as we walked down the street to the parkway and over to the beach. May 1, 1987—a date that I would forever remember for many reasons. The weather was warm enough for shorts and t-shirts. The sand was still warm from the hot day, and as the sun set, bonfires were built on the beach.

We drank the Apple Jack's, and Patrick took my hand. We walked down to a deserted end of the beach, and he stopped and sat down. He kissed me and laid me down in the sand. It felt perfect. The moon was full, and the sound of the waves lapping at the shore was the ideal soundtrack for the evening. I knew it was going to happen. This was my chance. His hands moved down my body and over my breasts. He lifted my shirt and kissed my nipples. His hands slipped down to my shorts and unzipped them. I reach my hands into his shorts and felt him growing firm through the fabric. He lowered his shorts, exposing himself to me. My inexperienced hands moved back and forth, not knowing how or what to do. He removed my clothes and climbed on top of me, kissing me gently. When he entered me, I was relieved. There was no pain. It felt nice. It seemed like the picture-perfect way to lose one's virginity. When he was done, we dressed and went back to the bonfire where others had gathered.

"Do you want to go out?" he asked.

"Yes," I laughed, assuming that was a given. I had no concept of a one-night stand. We walked home hand in hand, and I was content. Our night could have been scripted for a movie; it seemed so perfect.

After catching the bus to take me back to reality and the projects, I went to sleep peacefully.

On Monday, when we were back at school, Elaine was hungry for details, but Kara didn't want to hear anything about her brother. Since we were still in junior high and Patrick was in high school, I didn't see him all week but eagerly awaited the following weekend.

Saturday night, I was back at Kara's house to watch movies with her and Patrick. I sat beside him, cuddled against his chest. Kara was in the room but on another chair in front of us. Patrick unzipped his pants and moved my head down. He was gentle and had no idea, but as his hand pushed my head up and down, I was back on that couch with Chris, just a little girl, confused and betrayed. He was in my mouth for what seemed like a very long time and finally released. I was there only to pleasure him and nothing else. After I left that night, we never spoke again. We didn't break up. We didn't fight. He just ignored me. I suppose I ignored him, too. I don't know if I reacted strangely at that moment, and he sensed something was wrong. I'm fairly certain he had asked me out just to be the nice guy or perhaps out of guilt. I don't blame him. I don't really think he did anything unusual for guys at the time. I consented completely. I was just completely oblivious of the implications of sex.

By the time summer came, I was ready for a break from school. I wondered what was wrong with me. I had had sex in May and hadn't been with a guy since. On television, the adults always complained about not having sex often enough. I assumed that having regular sex proved I was desirable. Now the internal self-talk questioned everything.

Maybe no one wants me. Maybe I'm not pretty. Maybe I'm really weird. Maybe I will be alone forever. Maybe nothing I did was ever good enough.

I was often alone when I was at home. My friends all lived close to the school, and no one wanted to travel all the way to my house, not that I blamed them. I didn't really want anyone at my house anyway. My friends all came from middle-income families and had nice houses. My neighbourhood was the poor part of town and was known for crime. The only person in my neighbourhood that I really kept in touch with was my next-door neighbour, Julie. We didn't spend a lot of time together, but occasionally she came over, and I would cut and perm her hair, or we'd try out new makeup or just sit and listen to music. It was early August, and I went to her house to watch movies with Julie and Ken, her brother. I'd always thought he was cute, but he was three years older than me and usually stayed away from us. He was probably too cool to hang out with his little sister and her friend.

When we were younger, we did play together sometimes. The most memorable time was when their mom got a new fridge, and Julie and I made the fridge box into a fort where the three of us played house. In that box, he gave me my first kiss. Now, fourteen years old and sitting next to him in their basement, the tingle of hormones took over, and before I knew it, he kissed me. Julie had fallen asleep, and one thing led to another. Then he was on top of me, and I went along with it. That's what you did, right? No big deal. It was just sex, after all. We had sex twice that summer, but I had no preconceived notions that we were dating and zero expectations. I had learned that lesson.

That summer, my grandparents rented a cottage on Graham Lake and invited Mom and me. The small wood plank cottage sat among several other cottages in the middle of an RV campground. There were two small bedrooms and an open living area with a kitchen. Most of the people on the lake knew one another, having been camping there year after year for most of their lives. I brought my Walkman and favourite cassettes, which included Bruce Springsteen, Bon Jovi, Bryan Adams, and Corey Hart, with the intention of sitting in the sun for hours replaying my cassettes, tanning, and generally being an angsty teenager. Plans changed when I was introduced to a few of the regular campers. There was a boy named David, who was my age, and he proved to be the perfect escape from my grandfather, who always seemed to be lingering just a little too close. Most of the kids were younger, and David was happy to ditch the little ones and go off exploring.

    David showed me around the grounds. Several RV campers were lined up one after the other, with people who came to the campground every year. His own family camped here all summer, and his mother would commute to work on weekdays. He showed me the paths that snaked around the shallow lake and the dock, just out of sight of the main campground. We watched a heron standing in the reeds and listened to the loons call out across the water at dusk. We ended the evening sitting around the campfire, roasting marshmallows, enjoying the simplicity of a warm summer night. The next day, he came by early and had breakfast with us. We swam in the lake and laid out, drying ourselves in the sun. After lunch, we went for a walk, and he took me down a shaded meadow path, where he reached over and took my hand. He was sweet and gentle.

    "This is really nice," he said as he looked away shyly. When we sat by the edge of the lake, and when he leaned over to kiss me, it was a simple kiss on the lips: no open mouth, no tongue, no roving hands clutching at my breasts. When evening came, around the campfire, he put his arm around me. My grandfather, Nanny, and Mom were there, and I noticed a raised eyebrow from Mom.

    "I don't want you to leave," he whispered as he leaned in and kissed my cheek. I still had five days left, and I knew what should come next. He would want to get me alone, and we'd have sex. That was the goal, and if a boy didn't want to have sex with me, it meant he didn't really love me.

The next day, as I came back from spending the morning with David, my grandfather slipped something into my hand. It wasn't a twenty-dollar bill this time. It was three condoms.

"I'll take your Nanny and Mom for a long walk this afternoon so you can have the cottage to yourself," he said with a grin. This man was facilitating his fourteen-year-old granddaughter's sex life, and he found some sort of perverse pleasure in it. I did not bring David to the cottage that afternoon.

I'm not doing what he tells me to do. That's just gross. My grandfather doesn't get to dictate when I have sex. I have my own condoms anyway.

Kara, Elaine, and I had bought some a few months before, just in case.

Two days later, David and I went for another walk in the woods. We stopped in a grassy spot in the sun and sat down. I kissed him, and I moved my hands down his body and made my intentions known. My hands went into his shorts and around him, soon stroking him gently. I did what I thought I was supposed to do with a guy. I took off my shorts and pulled him onto me, helping him move inside of me. It was over quickly, and I worried I had done something wrong. Looking back, I realize that it was probably his first time, and I felt bad. I don't think this was what he wanted. I had no concept of a relationship with a guy that didn't include sex. My grandfather had encouraged me, and David went along with it. I was doing what girls did to have boyfriends and be liked or maybe even loved.

Later that day, David and I were back at the cottage, arms

wrapped around each other, laying in the late sun on the deck. There was a man in a small fishing boat out in the middle of the lake. I'd heard the lake was only six to eight feet deep and not very wide, so when he accidentally flipped out of the boat, I expected to see him go down, bounce back up and swim to shore. Instead, he came back up a few times, but it seemed he couldn't swim. He flailed his arms around, and the small motorboat began circling him.

"He doesn't know how to swim," someone yelled. People began to gather on shore, and a few tried to start their boats to go the short distance, but none of the boats would start. I stood among a group of adults just staring at the man slowly drowning. I had the urge to jump into the water and swim out to the drowning man. Thoughts swirled through my head.

Why wasn't anyone doing anything? I want to do something. Am I allowed to do something? Would I get in trouble if I jumped in the water? Better stay here, or I might make things worse. But he's drowning, and no one is doing anything.

All of these adults and not a single person moved. After the boat circled him several times, it hit him in the head, and he went down under the water one last time. There was a hush and pause over the crowd as we collectively held our breath, waiting for him to reappear at the surface of the water. We had all watched a man die, and no one did anything to stop it.

Some people had thought to start their own boats and try to reach him. But, some strange karmic thing happened, and not a single boat would start. The police and an ambulance eventually arrived. For the next few hours, as the sun set and darkness crept into the evening, police boats searched up and down the lake for the man's body. I kept imagining that he would be found farther along the shore, somehow miraculously alive. They finally stopped searching for the night and returned the next morning. His body was found exactly where he had gone down, right in front of our cottage, in just over six feet of water. They dragged his swollen and sullen gray body to shore. This was my first experience with death, and it repeatedly ran through my mind like a movie playing at the theatre, running on a loop.

Helplessness weighed me down. Maybe I could have done something. I could have jumped in and maybe saved him, but I had been too scared. If all these adults hadn't done anything, why should I think I could have? It haunted me for some time to come, the memory of his arms coming up, grasping for the help that would never arrive, and the quiet whir of his little fishing boat motor.

For the remainder of the week, David and I were inseparable. David only knew the man who had died in passing, but still, he was quiet, and his gaze would linger across the lake. When I left at the end of the week, we promised to write often, and we did for a few months. We would talk on the phone periodically, but the long-distance charges were expensive. As summer turned to fall, I started high school. My letters and calls decreased. David called more frequently, but often I was out or didn't have time to talk as homework piled on. That week at Graham Lake felt like a story in someone else's life, and I had to focus on my real life.

Then, one weekend it was as if David came crashing into my reality. He called every few minutes. He wanted to know why I hadn't written and if I was seeing another guy. He asked me question after question, and eventually, I stopped answering the phone. My mom got mad at me as if I had done something wrong. Somehow it was my fault he was harassing me. She took the phone off the hook for the rest of the night so we could sleep, but it began again the next day. I'm not sure if she called back and spoke to his parents or what happened, but the calls eventually stopped. David and that sweet summer affair weren't reality, but he didn't seem to understand that. We lived too far apart, and life went on. It was just sex after all, but maybe it was something more for him.

Had I hurt him? Was I a bad person? Was I just like Chris?

chapter 7

Grade Nine meant a new school and a lot of change. It felt like there was an expectation to grow up and be responsible young adults. After a summer of learning about relationships and the new pressures of high school, I was just existing and going through the motions each day. I was no longer trying to stand out and be the centre of attention with provocative clothes. I was quite happy to fly under the radar.

Perhaps that girl who wanted all the attention was a slut and had asked for it. Maybe it had all been my fault. Maybe I was just like Chris, and I don't want that.

In a school that was overcrowded, the sea of kids would move through the hallways, and at only five feet tall, I was literally swept up in it, seeing nothing but people's shoulders and backs as I struggled to get to my next class. I was invisible, and that was okay.

From the very beginning of high school, I had a free period to do as I pleased. There were no restrictions except that we couldn't be in the halls disturbing classes in session. I thought myself lucky to share a free period with Clinton, a boy that had been in my class since grade one, even though we had never been close friends. Most of the time, we sat on the front steps of the old building and chatted about this and that. Elaine would regularly ask me what we talked about, what he liked, and if he was interested in anyone. I knew she'd had a crush on him since sixth grade.

    Soon, Clinton started hanging out with us more often, and one day, when school was cancelled due to burst water pipes, we all went to Elaine's house and to the basement to watch television and have a couple of drinks. I poured a few concoctions from the miscellaneous bottles of alcohol I found in the cupboard. Elaine had disappeared off into another part of the house. Despite knowing her feelings for Clinton, when he kissed me and took me into the other room, I followed along. Clinton was a normal guy, from a normal family, and apparently, he liked me. I would let him do anything he wanted. I would do anything I thought he might like. I was with Clinton when Elaine came downstairs, looking for us. She walked in, then turned right back around and went to her room. If I had stopped for just a second to think about it, I would have known that it was a bad idea, but another part of me wanted nothing more than the validation that I was wanted by, not only any boy but one of the popular guys who had lots of friends. Elaine was rightfully hurt and upset, but she didn't seem to get mad at me.

    Elaine, Kara, and I had our share of the usual teenage girl drama. Things became awkward with Clinton, and we spent less time together. Kara broke up with her boyfriend and started dating a new guy. Elaine still wanted to be with Clinton, but he had absolutely no interest, and I thought I needed a boyfriend to fit in. I wanted to be good enough that some boy would like me. I wanted to be smart and pretty, but since that didn't seem to be possible, I wanted to blend in and be invisible because then I couldn't be hurt.

    I struggled between my desire to be invisible and receive attention from the boys to validate my existence. Thinking blondes were prettier, I started lightening my dark brown hair, first with lemon juice, which didn't do much, then eventually with blonde hair dye. No one I knew went to a salon to get their hair dyed. That was something rich people did. My mom had used a boxed product for years, so I thought to do the same.

Each time I dyed my hair, it would get a little lighter, and I thought it looked great, perhaps a lovely caramel blonde. The first time I really saw myself was when I received my photo ID for my bus pass. My hair was orange. It was awful. I didn't know that I needed to bleach my dark hair first before dyeing it blonde, and no one ever said anything. I hadn't succeeded in looking prettier, and I was not invisible with this hideous hair colour. That very day I went to the store and found a beautiful sable brown dye that was rich and luxurious in the picture on the box. Once home, I applied the dye, and thirty minutes later, as I rinsed it out and dried my hair, I was horrified. My hair appeared black, especially against my pale skin. I went to school one day, and even though one of the popular girls complimented me, I felt like a vampire. This was the goth look before that was a thing people did. I ended up staying home a couple of days and dyed my hair two more times that same week with lighter colours trying to get something close to my natural brown. My mom never said a word. She seemed not even to notice. Maybe she did, and I was no longer listening.

I didn't know who to listen to or go to for advice and help. My mom wasn't someone that I would confide in, as I never had in the past, always hiding my secrets from her, trying to protect her.

Why would I talk to her now?

Like many teenagers, my friend's opinions were the most

important. I often talked to Elaine about my ongoing crush on Kyle, the boy I had spent hours talking to on the phone.

"Do you want me to ask him if he likes you?" Elaine offered. I agreed, wanting to know once and for all, but I was also scared to find out the truth. At long last, I would know whether there was a chance. I was by Elaine's locker, waiting for her to return, talking about plans for the weekend with other students from our grade. I could soon see Elaine talking with him down the hall. With my anticipation building, I then watched her approach me, hoping that he might want me.

"He said you have a good body, but he doesn't like your face," she told me, shaking her head. Everything stopped for a second. Voices around me blurred. The way she told me was devastating. The tears pooled in my eyes, but I could not react, not here in the middle of all these people. I looked down, trying to compose myself as best I could.

"Thanks for talking to him for me," I said as I walked off.

Looking back, I sometimes wonder if it was true, if he had been so blunt and cruel or if she wanted me to hurt like she had been hurt when she saw me with Clinton. At the time, I believed what she said. The internal dialogue running in the back of my head took over. Sometimes I could keep it at bay, but now it was loud and clear.

Of course, it's true. Why would anyone want to date you? You're ugly. No one will ever want to be with you. You're not good enough.

It validated every fear I had. That night, in the darkness and solitude of my room, the tears flowed. I lay in bed, staring out the window. I wondered who I was. I had dreamt of Kyle driving up and taking me away, like a knight on a white horse, there to rescue me. That night, I gave up any dreams. I would never have a life like those I saw on television. There would be no husband or house and the safety and security that came with it.

There were a few more sexual experiences with guys as I tried to find someone, anyone who would like me. I was desperate to be accepted by men, even if it was by sleeping with them, but by the end of the year, I had nothing to show for it: no real boyfriend and no sense of acceptance by a guy.

Maybe I was doing something wrong? Maybe I didn't know how to satisfy a guy sexually? Maybe this was just one more area of my life that I was failing.

I shared my experiences with my closest friends.

Elaine said, "My mom says you're a human mattress."

I was incredibly hurt.

Was that all I was? Who says that about a fourteen-year-old girl? Who Doesn't see that there's something wrong and do something? And why would Elaine tell me about it? Maybe it was true, but I don't know why she was so cruel.

I now know she was battling her own demons through high school. I also know that as her friend, I didn't see or understand her struggles, and I wasn't there for her. We thought we shared everything, but in reality, we all had our secrets, those hidden, shameful parts of ourselves that never saw the light of day.

I struggled each day and tried to stay on the periphery so I would not be noticed. My mantra became, "If no one saw you there, they wouldn't reject you." Many of my friends, including Kara and Elaine, were in gifted programs and took enriched classes. Next to them, I always felt like I wasn't smart enough, and it reinforced the message I had gotten from Mom all along that I wasn't as good as she was. My grades weren't as good as her straight As, and they weren't as good as my friends'. I was dumb, and I was ugly. I would see Patrick, Kara's brother, in the halls at school, but he completely ignored me. I would run into Clinton sometimes, but we no longer talked. If any of the guys I had been with had treated me with a little respect or even acknowledged me after we'd had sex, maybe I would have maintained a thread of dignity. I was literally an object to be used and discarded. How I desperately wanted to be worthy of someone's attention.

Only my closest friends, Kara and Elaine, paid any attention to me. We often went to Elaine's house for sleepovers. Her mom was around but didn't interact with us at all. There was a cupboard above the fridge, and I would drag the barstool over to reach the bottles her mom kept there. We would pour ourselves large drinks into tall plastic cups, mostly straight alcohol, and head for the basement before her mom got home from work. One night, Elaine and Kara were drunker than I had ever seen. They were so sick; I'm sure they had alcohol poisoning. At one point, Elaine passed out in her own vomit, and I wondered if I should wake up her mother, who was just upstairs. I didn't want to get anyone in trouble, but I was also worried about her. Eventually, she came to enough so that I could move her and clean up. I always wondered how we didn't get caught. There was no way her mother didn't know we had been drinking. The smell of the basement itself would have given it away.

My drinking probably culminated when Elaine and I started working at a little pizza place. We would tell our mothers that we were working until close at 1:00 a.m., but in fact, we would be done work at 9:00 p.m. We'd have the rest of the night free to ourselves without parental interference. By the time we got home, they'd be in bed, so it seemed to be the perfect cover.

"Mike, can you pick up some Peach Schnapps for us?" we asked one of the pizza-delivery guys. Mike looked at the other delivery guy, who just shrugged and smirked. An hour later, between deliveries, Mike was able to pop into the liquor store and buy us what we wanted. At the end of our shift, we took the bottle of Peach Schnapps and walked down to the nearby woods. The air was crisp and chilly, and we found some brush and old newspaper flyers some kids had likely dumped to avoid their paper route. With a small lighter, we were able to get a tiny fire started. I pulled over a log to sit on, and we cracked open the bottle. The first few sips were harsh and burned, but soon we didn't notice and finished the rest of the bottle in just over forty-five minutes. We had nothing to put out the fire with, but it was so small that we could stomp it out with our shoes. I still worried that we'd set the forest on fire.

The trip back seemed much longer. We stumbled up the hill towards work. When we got to the main road, we had to cross, but I was on my hands and knees and crawled by this point. We needed to go back to work to get our school bags before going home.

I somehow got to my feet, and as we walked through the front door, we both stopped suddenly. The manager had dropped by to check on things.

"Hi Betty," I said as I stared at the floor and worked very hard to walk in a straight line to the staff area for my stuff. I hoped she hadn't noticed I was drunk.

What would happen if she knew? Don't act drunk. Don't act drunk. Don't act drunk.

Betty didn't say anything that I heard and left soon after. I figured I had played it cool. I sat down in the chair, just for a moment, waiting for Elaine to get her things. There was a pot of coffee brewing, and I decided that would help sober me up. I never drank coffee, but that evening, I poured a cup of straight, black coffee and took a sip. It was bitter and awful. Adding sugar seemed the logical answer, so then I drank the syrupy black liquid, hoping for some semblance of sobriety. Within a few minutes, I realized my mistake. Sugary coffee and Schnapps do not mix well. I spent the next hour on the floor in the staff washroom, next to the toilet. Any other time, I would have recovered enough to leave and find my way home. I might have even got a ride from the pizza-delivery guy, but this one evening, my mom decided to pick me up at work. Since I was supposed to be working until 1:00 a.m., she thought it would be nice if I didn't have to take the bus home. Mom walked in and stood by the counter at the front of the small storefront, while I was on the floor in the staff bathroom.

"She's really not feeling well. I think she got food poisoning when we grabbed food from the burger place," Elaine said to my mom, trying to cover for me. Mom didn't buy it. I got myself up and off the floor, wiped off my face, and managed to walk to the car. She drove me home in silence but never spoke of it.

My boss called me at home the next day to check on me, although I was still hungover and didn't register the call. I hadn't fooled anyone. Thinking I could was ridiculous considering I'd crossed the road on my hand and knees. I didn't get fired, which was hard to believe, but then she might have had to fire the other staff, some of whom were her own family, who had given two fourteen-year-olds alcohol. If the incident came out, I'm sure the head office may have even fired her. After this, I rarely drank, and a few months later, I quit my job.

It was probably for the best that I wasn't working as I entered grade ten. My classes were fun, and I did my homework more regularly. I had given up any hope that any of the boys would ever want to date me. I had no aspirations and no thoughts of what I would do after high school. University never really crossed my mind. I didn't know anyone who had gone, and no one in my family or neighbourhood had continued their education. I had no road map for after high school. I only knew that it was essential to get good grades and keep up with my friends.

Having not put much effort into school the last few years, I now had to buckle down to keep up with expectations of getting all As. This was also when I started getting migraines. I'd had a few when I was younger, but now I was getting them regularly. I'd seen my mom with headaches and migraines all her life, and now I started to know for myself what she experienced. I would get intense throbbing in my head. When I would stand up, the pulsing would worsen, and feel like someone was knocking on the inside of my skull. My mom was quite obliging, perhaps a bit too much. It became easy to stay home with a headache, even on days when I could have gone in and powered through. She would leave for her job cleaning houses, and I would have the house to myself for the day. I would sleep in and then watch television for the afternoon. I would return to school the next day but have missed a lot of work. Trying to catch up on notes, homework, and assignments was difficult. I was too shy to talk with teachers and was falling further and further behind.

The cycle continued for months, with more migraines, followed by a couple of missed days and an attempt to catch up. Some days, I would stay home after a migraine for an extra day, hoping I could just stay current with my classwork. I often wished

I could go back in time and start high school over to do just a little better. Sometimes I wished I could go back to grade one and do it all over. This time, maybe I would get it right. I'd had these thoughts since I was about nine, always wishing I could go back and start over. That seemed the only way I would ever dig myself out of this hole. By Christmas, I had missed so much school that my whole year was at risk.

    I had seen the doctor multiple times, tried a variety of medications and nothing seemed to help. I had good days where I could go to school, but then a migraine would strike again. Every time I got back up, it would beat me down again. I lost touch with my friends because while they were going out and having fun, I was stuck at home in a dark room, hoping the pain would end. Some medications worked, but the side effects would make me feel terrible. I was at the end of my rope and wanted an escape from the world. I didn't think I would ever catch up. After the doctor provided a note to justify the missed school days, the board of education provided tutors who would come to my home once a week to teach me lessons and give me homework. I didn't have to face school or the looks of disapproval from teachers. The last half of the year, I spent at home, not seeing friends, not going out, not doing much of anything beyond classwork. I guess I had finally managed to become invisible. No one saw me.

    Did my mom even see me?

    I liked the little bubble I had created. I lived in my own world, and my bedroom and living room became my safe space. I would watch the late afternoon re-runs and Thursday night sitcoms on television, and I had a cassette player with all the music I loved. That and schoolwork were my world. Mom came and went with her work cleaning houses, and I was on my own to do what I wanted. My grades improved, and I was finally enjoying learning.

Eventually, with the new medication and lots of rest, the migraines became manageable. By the following year, I went back to school. My friends knew I had been off with migraines, but I don't think anyone believed it was a real thing. They hadn't reached out to me, and it was like I was out of sight, out of mind. It was strange walking down the halls. I was now a junior, in grade eleven, and didn't feel so lost in the sea of kids. There were plenty of younger kids who wandered aimlessly, searching for their classes. My friends were polite, but I didn't get asked to sit with them at lunch or out on the weekends. Mostly, I sat by my locker, books open, doing homework. I'd arrive early in the morning and do homework in the classes that had heavy textbooks, so I didn't have to lug them home. At lunch, I'd eat by myself, content not to interact with people beyond pleasantries. No one bothered me, and I was able to stay hidden. No one ever wondered why I started getting migraines and why I withdrew from my friends. No one saw that maybe there was something deeper going on.

Staying hidden meant I stopped comparing myself to others, and something had changed within. Over the last year, I finally realized that I wasn't stupid. I was getting As in my classes. I had a new sense of confidence, and even if I didn't have anything else, I was smart enough. My tutors helped me feel like I was caught up and could face the new year. My teachers were kind, and I no longer got looks of disapproval. I still missed the occasional day, but overall, I finally felt like a normal student, albeit without a social life.

I was in a good space and wanted to make some money of my own, so I started a new part-time job, making almost double what I had at the pizza place. It was in a restaurant owned by a woman in the local mall, and she said she wanted to give a girl a chance as she had too many guys in the kitchen already. The kitchen was like a long corridor, starting with the sandwich section, then the grill and fryers, followed by the stoves, after which there was a line of fridges and a long counter with sinks at the end for prep. The first day I walked into the kitchen, Jon, the kitchen manager, walked me from one end to the other, opening every fridge door pointing out all the food items. I was lost and could hardly understand him through his thick Chinese accent. It took a few months before I started to understand him fully, and I'm lucky I managed to do well enough to keep the job. I was working two shifts during the week and most Saturdays. There was no Sunday shopping yet, so the mall was closed, and therefore, I had every Sunday off.

  The kitchen was where I met Glen. He started work at the restaurant about two months after me. He was almost seven years older, and one day, I worked up the courage to ask him out.

chapter 8

I'm not sure what changed. But that day, when Glen and I were working together, I decided to ask him out. The daytime staff were all much older adults who had worked together for years, and the evening part-time staff included three brothers who came from a patriarchal family, where men were listened to, and women did not disagree with them. With Glen, I found someone I could connect with. He had grown up in the local neighbourhood and had seen many of the same things I had in my neighbourhood. Crime, drugs, and abuse were a part of the landscape. Glen would talk about his years working in restaurants and how one day he would open his own. He had dreams, and I was intrigued. Toward the end of our shift, I asked him if I could buy him a beer at the local hole-in-the-wall bar, Crackers.

"They won't serve you," was all he said.

"I'll just have ginger ale," I responded. With that, he agreed. Although I usually always drank Coke, I guess I wanted to seem more mature, and Ginger Ale sounded more mature.

Crackers was a small restaurant, with the tiny storefront windows covered in black, so once inside, the day disappeared, and we were lost in the neverending night. Occasionally, there would be live music, but mostly it was just the local watering hole for the surrounding neighbourhoods. I sat down with Glen at a small table at the front. This vantage point provided me with the opportunity to study him more closely. He was six feet tall and had a lean build. His wavy hair was a strange blonde. The roots were darker, but the ends were almost a white blonde. Glen explained that when he was younger, his family lived up north, and his hair would go completely white-blonde in the summer months when daylight lasted almost twenty-four hours.

"Hey, Glen," the waitress said, coming over to our table.

"Hi, Christine," he replied, "I'll have a beer." I felt a little uncomfortable as she smiled and mildly flirted with Glen.

Had they gone out, or was she just being a friendly waitress looking for a decent tip?

"It's ladies' night! You get a free shooter," she said, turning to me. I guess they were going to serve me after all.

"I'll have a rum and Coke," I said.

"And the shooter?" she asked.

"Surprise me," I replied. Glen raised an eyebrow but said nothing. As we talked through the evening, I marvelled at this man. He had muscular, strong arms, likely from years working in restaurant kitchens. His blonde hair fell just a little long over his ears and was brushed back on top, showing hints of a receding hairline. He had a rugged look, not clean-cut like the boys at my school. His blue eyes followed mine, and he listened when I spoke. At the end of the night, he was a perfect gentleman and walked me home. This would be the first of many evenings out together.

Glen didn't take me out on grand romantic dates. Almost everything we did was within walking distance of my home. We saw the occasional movie at the theatre two blocks away, and we would stop in at the nearby arcade, where he would play games for what felt like hours on end. I was terrible at video games, and my quarter would last but a minute. It didn't take long until I introduced Glen to my mom. I had talked about him to her but never mentioned his age.

"How old is he?" she had asked.

"He's around twenty. I'm not sure exactly. I never asked," I said vaguely. At seventeen, I figured twenty wouldn't be too objectionable. He was, in fact, twenty-three. The first time they met, she talked to him, and they realized they had both gone to the same high school. They shared stories and even had a few of the same teachers. It was a little weird to have my mom and boyfriend with things in common.

"How old is he really?" she asked after they met.

"He's twenty-three," I finally confessed.

"What is a twenty-three-year-old doing with a teenager?" she asked, obviously not impressed.

"We have fun together, and he's really nice to me," I replied.

He actually likes me, and I don't feel bad about myself when I'm with him. Why can't she just be happy for me? Why can't she just leave me alone? I have finally found someone who didn't just want sex but wanted to spend time with me.

Mom did not forbid me from seeing him. However, there were suddenly stricter curfews now at seventeen than when I was fourteen. I had to be home by eleven, and she would be in bed when I got home, so I wouldn't know if she heard me come in late until the next morning.

"You were late getting home last night," she said sternly.

"It was like three minutes after eleven."

"Late is late. I don't care if it's one minute. You will be home on time, or you won't be going out," Mom yelled.

"That's ridiculous," I yelled back, storming up to my room and slamming the door. After an argument, Mom would give me the silent treatment, and I would do the same. It was like a game of chicken to see who would speak first, and sometimes almost a week would pass before we spoke. She often gave in and would start talking to me as if nothing had happened. There was never any resolution to our fights.

We didn't fight all the time, though, and that summer, Mom planned a trip for the two of us. We went camping for a week, just a mother and a daughter. We had a great time. We drove to a campground, set up our tent, and either explored the landscape or laid on the beach. Then we packed up, moved to the next campground, and set up again. I found it hard not to talk to Glen. I felt disconnected and worried as this was the first boyfriend that lasted for any length of time.

Would anything change in the week I was gone?

Mom decided to go to a motel halfway through the week, so we could have a good night's sleep and have a hot shower. I was thrilled because I would be able to find a payphone and call Glen.

"You don't need to call him. You're too attached to this guy," she said, ridiculing me. "I don't know that this is a good relationship for you. I'm not sure he's a good influence, and he is way too old," she went on and on. Instead of this being a trip to help us bond, it started to feel like a trip to get me away from Glen. Sometimes over the years, I have wished she had told me not to see him, but she was alone, raising a teenager with no outside support and probably worried it would push me farther away. I often obsessed over certain points in my life and how much different my life would have been. If she had forbidden me from seeing Glen, maybe I would have gone to university and had an easier life. Today, I no longer think this. I know everything

I've experienced has made me who I am.

Back at home, Mom continued to try to get me to spend time with my grandfather.

"Nanny would appreciate it if you went with your grandfather to the nature trail. She doesn't like him going alone. She's worried he might fall or get hurt."

How in the hell did it become my responsibility to make sure he was safe when he went out?

"Mom, I don't want to go," I said.

"You are so ungrateful. Your grandfather has done so much for you, and now you walk away like he doesn't exist," she uttered, angry with me again. That afternoon, I sat down at my typewriter and began typing out all my anger and hurt.

She doesn't understand anything about me. Mom doesn't know anything. I've hidden his secrets from her all these years. Where did it get me?

In that letter, I told her how my grandfather had given me adult magazines and a vibrator. I wrote about him masturbating in front of me. I shared how Chris had sexually abused me. I wrote and wrote for four pages. With each page, a weight lifted and strength emerged. I wasn't hiding in the corners but instead standing a little taller. I was no longer going to hide things to protect others. I was shedding the shame and fears about being caught. I was holding my head high, knowing none of this was my fault, and I was not going to be forced into doing anything I did not want to do ever again.

Later that day, Glen came over, and I let him read the letter.

"I don't want to talk about it. She wants to know why I won't go with my grandfather. Now she will know," I said. There was a lot of anger pulsing through my body. I folded the letter neatly in thirds and left it on the kitchen table, then Glen and I went out. I had no shame about any of it. I knew Mom would be devastated. I had spent years hiding this from her. Maybe I wanted to hurt her like I had been hurt. Maybe then she would finally understand and leave me alone.

When I came home later that day, Mom was sitting in the living room, waiting for me with the letter in her hand. Time slowed as I took in the room. I noticed for the first time how much she had aged. Her dyed blonde hair was dry and frizzy, and her skin was pale and papery. This appearance was a sure sign she had a migraine. Her blue eyes looked grayer. The small living room appeared even smaller, filled to the brim with furniture, bookshelves filled with her prized books, and every inch of wall space covered with prints, photos, and artwork. The world shrunk at this moment, the one I had both longed for and dreaded for so long. I wanted to disappear and wished it all away, but I had opened Pandora's box and was about to find out what would come out.

"What do you want to do?" she asked.

"Nothing. I don't want anyone to know. I only wrote this so you would understand."

"But I need to talk to Grandpa about this," she said quietly.

"No!"

She doesn't understand. That would ruin everything. She is missing the point. This isn't about telling everyone. It was about her understanding me.

"I need to say something. We can't just leave this," she went on. Mom talked to me for what felt like hours, and I have no idea what she said. It was all a jumble of unrecognizable words. My brain shut down.

She wants to tell. She wants to expose me. She would ruin everything. What would Nanny think if she found out? No! No! No! This was all wrong.

But I gave in. Mom wore me down and got what she wanted. Disclosure rule number one: Listen to what the victim wants and needs when they disclose. So much for that. We went over to Nanny and Grandpa's, and she handed him the letter. After he had read it, he handed it to my grandmother. I watched my letter be handed to Nanny and was absolutely crushed.

This absolutely can't be happening.

I will never understand why he gave it to my grandmother. *What good could come of it?*

"What are you going to do about it?" Nanny asked my mom.

"I don't know," Mom responded.

"Well, what about Chris? What are you doing about him?" Nanny asked. Mom had a quizzical look cross her face. She didn't seem to understand the question.

"What do you mean? What about Chris?" Mom said.

What do you mean? What doesn't she get? Nanny is asking what you are going to do about your ex-boyfriend who sexually abused me.

I think she read the letter, but after getting through the parts about her father, it was as if she didn't register the rest. We went home with nothing resolved. I felt worse because I now felt like she hadn't read the whole letter. I'm sure she did, but she went into shock.

I don't know if it was days or weeks later, but I was called to the school office. There was a message that I had a doctor's appointment. It was strange, but I didn't think much of it. I took the bus from school and walked into the appointment alone. The doctor appeared concerned. I thought maybe I was there for my yearly physical but sitting on his desk was the letter I had written. Nanny had brought it to him. The colour washed from my face. I sat down in the chair, staring down at his desk and that damn letter. The lights in the room suddenly seemed too bright. The doctor spoke, but it sounded muffled. I was in shock that my private letter, for my mom only, had made the rounds and was now sitting in this virtual stranger's hands. The doctor gave me a referral for counselling services, and I was sent off to go home. On the bus ride home, I had a mix of anger and relief. I was angry that my letter had been shared, but I had a sense of relief that I would have someone to talk to that might understand because, apparently, no one in my family did.

    I soon realized that I might have overestimated how helpful a counsellor would be. I went exactly twice. Once, alone to meet the counsellor who, after I spilled out all my story, asked if I would rather see a female therapist.

    "No, I'm good," I replied and booked another appointment. I didn't really care who I was telling. It felt so good to get it all off my chest. Glen came along for the second appointment as the therapist had suggested, knowing I was dating. Most of the session was spent talking about safe sex and AIDS. This seemed completely unrelated to why I was there, but considering it was the height of the AIDS epidemic, I'm guessing that many services were using every opportunity to educate the public about the dangers. It was unfortunate timing, though, because it felt like the therapist wasn't listening to me. I merely wanted to share my story, be told that it was okay and that I hadn't done anything wrong. All I got was that the unprotected sex I was having with my boyfriend, the only person I felt safe with, was bad. I never returned.

There are many different therapists out there, and it can take a few tries to find the right one, but at the time, I was disheartened by the process. At least Mom stopped trying to force me to spend time with my grandfather. I can't imagine what it felt like for her to know that her daughter had been abused by people she trusted. I can only imagine the guilt and perhaps shame that would come with something like this. It isn't uncommon for parents to blame themselves, but I don't really know how she felt, as we never talked about it. I didn't end up talking to anyone about it. I disclosed what happened but didn't get the opportunity to process how it affected me, so I pushed it aside and went on with my life.

By the time I was in grade twelve, my migraines were back with a vengeance, and I again withdrew from school and had tutors help me finish my year. I somehow managed to work a few shifts at the restaurant and see Glen, but I regressed a bit from the world. Even though I wasn't going to school, no one seemed to link the abuse with my migraines and my inability to go to school. During my first bout with migraines when I was sixteen, I also suffered from depression. This time, it was more indifference about everything, and migraines were my crutch.

I didn't care what anyone thought. I did my own thing, and no one was going to tell me what to do or how to do it. I had eight teachers, a guidance counsellor, and vice principal all involved with my situation. I had my mom, grandparents, family, the doctor, and a therapist. Somehow, even with all these adults around, no one stopped to see what was going on with me.

How did I fall through the cracks? How was it that I was

left to my own devices?

I know counselling wasn't discussed as much back then, but somehow, someone should have done more. I'd like to say things are better today, but in some families, sexual abuse continues to be swept under the rug.

In my family, the sexual abuse was ignored. The aunts and my cousins who knew didn't seem to believe it could be as bad as I said. I'm not sure what they heard because they didn't talk to me. No one in my family talked about anything of any substance. When Christmas rolled around, I was at my grandparents' house with all the family, like every other year before, as if nothing had happened. My anger, my hurt, and my confusion were not important and were better ignored. Everyone wanted things to go back to normal. Police were never involved because I had made it clear I didn't want anyone to know. If they had been, perhaps I would have had more support, but in my neighbourhood and in my family, we didn't trust the police; after all, they were the ones who arrested my mother.

chapter 9

The strained relationship with my mom continued. She always seemed angry whether I was a couple of minutes late for curfew or if I wanted to spend part of the weekend with Glen instead of doing something with her. I started to check out. I was no longer present in that house. I wanted out. I didn't want to be around my family, and I didn't want to live at home with my mom, who was being unreasonable. I started apartment hunting and toured at least six apartment buildings in the area but had to figure out how I could make a little more money to afford the rent and other costs. I also needed to outfit the apartment, so I started buying housewares when they were on sale.

    Within about six months, I had dishes, glasses, pots and pans, kitchen linen, cutlery, serving utensils, can opener, toaster, and kettle. I even bought a coffee maker, though I didn't drink coffee, because I might want it for guests. My very first purchase had been a set of four really nice wine glasses; that made me feel grown-up. I came home week after week with a new box or bag of stuff for an apartment and piled it into the closet where I used to hide the adult magazines and vibrator from my grandfather. But this time, I wasn't hiding it. If Mom had opened my closet, she would have seen it stacked top to bottom with everything I would need to live on my own. I saved money from my job, too, so that I would have enough to buy some furniture when the time came to move out.

The house felt smaller, like it was closing in around me. There wasn't a room that didn't have a traumatic event associated with it—from my room with memories of crying myself to sleep while Chris and my mom fought to sexual abuse in their bedroom, the living room, and basement. There was the fear associated with mom's stalker banging on our door and breaking the glass while we waited for police to come. I tried to remember the happy moments, but they were overpowered by so much that I couldn't forget.

I kept myself busy with work, school, and Glen, and I think as a result, Mom and I argued less often. I was hardly home, and so it almost seemed as though our relationship had improved. I decided to hold off on the apartment hunt for the time being and continued saving as much money as I could. This did sometimes put me at odds with Glen, who never seemed to have money.

"Let's go see a movie," I suggested.

"That would be great. I'm a little short of cash. Can you cover it this time?" he asked, knowing I would. Mostly, our dates were boring. We were more like a couple of teenagers hanging out together. He'd drop by, and we would walk to the local store, where he would proceed to play arcade games while I stood beside him watching. There was an arcade across from the movie theatre, and we would go in almost every time we walked by it. I dreaded it as Glen would play a game, and it would go on for a long time while I stood by waiting. I was bored and didn't enjoy video games that much.

Why did I put up with it? Why did I just stand around waiting on him?

Other dates involved taking the bus out to the suburbs and going to Glen's house, where he still lived with his parents. We'd walk the neighbourhood, hang out at the corner store where he played yet more video games, and occasionally he would bring along some alcohol that we would drink in the park. Other days we would walk over to his friend's apartment, and I would sit while they smoked weed. Their apartment was on the first floor, and people would come to the window, climb in, and buy weed and hash from them. Apparently, this was safer as they didn't want the security cameras at the front door, seeing too many people coming and going.

Glen smoked a lot of hash, but I didn't realize how much until one day, he asked me to front him some cash so he could buy a larger quantity that he could then resell while getting his own at cost. He said he would pay me back, plus give me a part of the profits. At the time, I didn't realize that I could have easily been arrested if he had been caught, and it came out that I funded his enterprise. I didn't really understand what I was doing or the potential consequences. Of course, I never saw much of the money back, as he ended up smoking most of it himself. I learned quickly not to trust him with money.

There were a few memorable dates, like the time we went to Capone's, a local Italian restaurant with white linen tablecloths, wine glasses on the table, and exquisite pasta. Glen talked about dreams for his own restaurant, and we brainstormed plans for a couple of different concepts. Later, when we went home, we sketched out ideas, floor plans, and menu ideas. Glen had dreams, and I was more than willing to tag along and dream someone else's dream. I had none of my own. I didn't know who I was and had no identity.

There were also a few dates I would rather forget. On my birthday, Glen was taking me out, and I was excited to be treated to dinner. When he arrived at the house, he was in the usual scruffy jeans, t-shirt, and baseball cap over his hair.

I guess we are going somewhere casual.

We started walking, and he said we were going to the local pizza place. It was essentially a storefront with half a dozen tables along the window.

"I don't have any cash. I'll get you back next time," he informed me halfway there. The disappointment crushed me. He had a job and lived at home with minimal expenses, yet I would be paying for my birthday meal. It was my birthday, and I wanted to feel special–like someone cared about me. Instead, we sat across from one another in cheap metal chairs and ate pizza that I was paying for, while Glen complained about his job, the weather, and the government. Glen had a way of blaming others for his problems. I tried to be supportive and listen to his plights with the world. The problem was he never seemed to do anything to help himself.

Eventually, Glen quit his job at the mall restaurant where we had met. He landed a full-time job at a new restaurant that was opening nearby. It was interesting as he talked about setting up a brand-new restaurant, the training schedules, and the excitement of working with the four new restaurant owners. The best part was that there were lots of hours to go around, so he made more money. Within a month of opening, I applied for a job there too. It was summer, and I worked full-time hours, saving a ton of money. I worked prep in the back of the kitchen, and days started at 8:00 a.m. with washing and breaking up case after case of iceberg lettuce for salads. Sometimes, we would prep several hundred heads of lettuce. We made pizza dough and cooked hundreds of pounds of pasta that had to be weighed out and individually portioned into little plastic bags. It was tedious work. There were vegetables to be washed and cut and meat to be pre-cooked.

The work was intensely busy as the summer season was in full swing, and the new restaurant, with a beautiful patio, quickly became a popular spot for locals. The people that I worked with were much closer to my age, and it had a party atmosphere. I suddenly had a whole new group of friends, something I hadn't had in a while. After hours, the owners would buy staff drinks, and we'd often be there until 2:00 in the morning.

As summer wound down, I had to go back to school. I was hardly home and rarely saw my mom. I had four courses to finish off high school. I needed six OAC, or grade thirteen courses, to apply for university, and I already had two. I managed to get the courses scheduled in the morning. My day would begin with a four-mile bike ride to school, class from 9:00 to 11:45 a.m., then a six and a half-mile bike ride to the restaurant where I would work from 12:30 p.m. until either 5:00 p.m. and often until 7:00 or 8:00 p.m. when I would bike another two and a half miles home. I'd do homework, go to bed, and repeat the next day. I did this for three to four days a week, plus worked most Saturdays and Sundays.

After two months and with the coming winter, I knew this wasn't sustainable. I would need to start taking the bus once the snow came, and that would add significant time to my commute. As Glen and I continued to talk about opening a restaurant, I realized that a college program for hotel and restaurant management would be far more beneficial. I didn't need the four courses I was taking. One English credit was required for me to graduate, and the class was available by correspondence. I could work at my own pace, at home, and could drop out of school.

I wasn't close with my old school friends, and I never thought about what I'd be missing by not being part of the graduating class.

I went to school, filled out the forms, and since I was now eighteen, I didn't need a parent's signature. I met with the guidance counsellor, who asked about my plan and stamped the form. It was done. The guidance counsellor didn't have any other questions. There were no suggestions or other options offered, no encouragement to finish and graduate with my friends. There was no mention that I might want to keep my options open. In under ten minutes, I was able to, on a whim, drop out of high school.

I was happy to have a semi-normal life now that I wasn't going to school. I worked full-time and still had time with friends from work. The migraines had subsided almost completely. I formed a close bond with several of the guys in the kitchen. There weren't many women working in kitchens then, so I was surrounded by guys, which I liked. It fed my need for attention and my need to feel pretty enough. I was flirty and took the sexist jokes in stride, assuming that it made me one of the guys, part of the group.

I worked prep with two guys, Roger and Nathan, who were roommates, and I soon learned from Roger that Nathan was interested in me. He was shy and a sort of quiet, brooding type of guy, but I was intrigued by any guy that paid me any attention. He was not much taller than me but had broad, strong shoulders and chest and deep dark eyes. I hung out with him a bit, and he was very sweet. In many ways, he was like Glen, a little scruffy and rough around the edges, but he was kind and treated me like I was something special. I went over to Roger and Nathan's house a couple of times to have a few drinks, and Nathan played his guitar for me.

I began to notice that with Glen, I felt like more of a convenience, someone to have sex with, someone who would watch him play video games and follow him around. Also, I did not like that he was smoking a lot of drugs. One day, we headed to one of Glen's friend's houses. It was a nice-looking bungalow in the middle of a quiet residential neighbourhood. When we went down to the basement, I saw bags of cocaine. Not small amounts either. Then I saw that one of the guys had a gun. That was so far from my comfort zone. Sure, I knew this was going on in my neighbourhood, but sitting in that basement, I remembered every drug bust on every television show I had watched, where the police burst in, and everyone was arrested, or another drug dealer comes in and shoots everyone. Either way, I did not want to be a part of this. Glen thought nothing of it. It was no big deal. I knew something had to change. I later heard a rival drug dealer set fire to the house.

Nathan was quiet, and although he smoked weed, it was just a little, recreationally. Nathan made it clear he wanted a relationship. Even his roommate, Roger, was encouraging me to take the leap and give this new potential relationship a shot. I was with Nathan one evening, and he placed his hand on my leg. He leaned in and kissed me gently. My body fluttered with anticipation. He kissed me again, this time more passionately. I broke up with Glen the next evening. We were at work, and toward the end of our shift, I told him this just wasn't going to work. He went outside, and in anger, punched the brick wall with his bare fist. His hand bled, and I left. I was done with him.

"I love you. I can be better. I don't want to lose you," Glen pleaded with me the next day.

    I wanted to believe him. I had been with him for over a year and wanted this to work. I wanted something stable in my life, and as much as I cared for Nathan, the idea of starting a new relationship with someone I didn't know that well was more than I could handle. I wanted stability in my life, and I had that with Glen. I went back. I always went back.

chapter 10

Fall weather brought colder days and crisp, frosty mornings. Glen and I continued to work at the restaurant, often arriving early in the morning or working late into the evening. I rode my bike to and from work, even in the dark of night. I never thought much about safety and wearing jeans and a black jacket. I was invisible to most drivers on the road. One evening, I drove down a stretch of road that had no streetlights when a car passed by much too close. The car just touched my handlebar, but it was enough to throw me off the bike and onto the gravel shoulder. I got back up, dusted myself off, and continued on my way. I never realized how lucky I was or how close to death I could have been.

My life with Glen revolved around the restaurant and little else. Our friends were from work, and there was no time for outside activities, not that Glen had much interest in anything besides smoking pot. From my perspective, we were a normal young couple, having fun. By Christmas, we were in a good place, and the plan was to spend Christmas Eve with Glen's family for "Réveillon," the French-Canadian tradition of celebrating Christmas Eve. Traditionally, families would go to midnight mass, during which Santa would bring gifts. Families would then go home to a big meal, and the children would open their gifts, or at least that's how it was explained to me. They would be awake until the wee hours, often after 3:00 a.m., and would then sleep in and get up for a late Christmas Day brunch. My mom was invited to join in the festivities, and since Glen's family no longer did midnight mass, the evening would end a little earlier.

We gathered around the tree and opened gifts as everyone else watched. When it was my turn to receive a gift, Glen pulled a small box from the boughs of the Christmas tree and handed it to me. I opened the box to find a ring with a tiny diamond embedded in the band.

"Will you marry me?" he said.

"Yes," I answered easily. I didn't stop to think. He put the ring on my finger, and I was engaged because that's what I was supposed to do. I'd never say "No." I never said no to anyone. My mom was sitting in a chair, and she smiled, but awkwardly. Through that smile, I could see something in her eyes, almost terror.

Was she remembering her own failed marriage? Was she worried I was too young? Was she seeing all my potential evaporate before her as I got saddled with a husband and eventually a family?

This is the logical next step. This is what one is supposed to do. Find a good man, and then get married.

While I know at the time I was happy, and in love, or at least what I thought was love, now looking back, I struggle to recognize what we had between us that kept me in the relationship. I guess it was a way to get away from my childhood. Maybe it was a chance to move on. After all, Glen was a good man, and he came from a real family. His parents were still married and appeared to be living a happy life together. His mom was a short, plump French Canadian woman, with her infectious laugh and her occasional bursts into song, usually French opera. She would cook meals for the family, clean the house, and do laundry. She doted on them all.

Glen's older sister, who had been out on her own for a year, had moved back home so she could pay off her credit card bills before striking out again. They supported her when she needed it. She lived in the family home with her parents and Glen for years. She would never leave that house until forced to when both her parents died within a year of one another. She was in her mid-fifties when that reality hit, and she would need to live on her own for the first time in over thirty years.

Glen's dad had worked for the Federal Government in the engineering field, although he was not an engineer. He looked like a grandpa with his greying beard and glasses perched on the end of his nose. He wore jeans, held up by suspenders that went up over his plaid shirt and round belly. He was always fixing something or noodling in the basement on one project or another.

He was overshadowed by his own father, who was very much the patriarch of the family and decided he was moving in with them. The grandfather told them what to do and decided on a house that he helped them buy to move out of their old neighborhood that was degrading quickly as crime increased. Glen's mom never seemed completely happy with the arrangement, but I'm not sure she had much to say in the matter. Glen's grandfather was a thin yet strong man who could build anything. He was from the east coast, where men worked with their hands and would pull themselves up by their bootstraps, or at least that was the image portrayed. He spent hours in the dust-covered basement cutting and sanding wood to build various pieces of furniture, but his prized project was his steam engine. He machined every piece and every gear himself in that very basement, although he never got the chance to complete the project.

    Glen's grandfather had a lot of hobbies that included making apple cider that was saved for special occasions. He would pull out one bottle and give everyone in the family a small glass, not much more than a taste, really. I was often seated next to him at family dinners, and he would usually have a second bottle stashed under the table with which he would fill his and my glass a few more times. I got a little tipsy from his apple cider on more than one occasion. This was a real family, and I was joining them. I would be part of something normal that didn't have hidden baggage. I was getting married and would have stability, love, and kindness. These were people who could take care of their family when things went wrong.

    Mom went home Christmas Eve, feigning happiness for the newly engaged couple, although I could see her unease. I stayed over and awoke early Christmas morning, not sure how I would get home. We were far out into the suburbs, and bus service was spotty with holiday schedules in place. Luckily, a family friend had also stayed over, and we shared a cab so that I could get home at a respectable time. Although Glen's dad had offered to drive me home on Christmas Day, I knew the family would not be awake for hours. Despite the cab ride, it was still a little after 10:00 a.m. when I arrived home. My mom was visibly disappointed. We always did Christmas morning gift opening early. Instead, for the first time since I had been born, she awoke alone to a quiet house, except perhaps the sound of her cats meowing for breakfast.

    We made our morning tea and opened presents, but there wasn't the usual glee. Christmas had always been the highlight of the year. We had a large fresh tree, decorations hung across every inch of the house, and the windows sparkled with coloured lights. Baking was done over several weeks leading up to Christmas. This was a day when everything had to be perfect at home. The house would be clean and spotless. Laundry would be all washed, and linen on the beds was fresh. Closets would be cleaned, and drawers organized. However, my engagement put a pallor over this goal for perfection.

Mom didn't mention the engagement, and when we saw the rest of the family later that day, there was no happy announcement. As we had dinner at Nanny and Grandpa's with all the family mulling around, I shared my news with a few people, and Mom stayed silent on the subject. When she was happy or excited about something, everyone knew. She would get giddy and bubbly. She was not happy. I was eighteen, a month shy of my nineteenth birthday, and I'm sure she felt like I was throwing my life away.

What does she know? She doesn't understand these things. I know exactly what I'm doing. It's time to go out on my own and become my own person, with Glen.

As I look back, I laugh at myself at my naivety.

Christmas passed, and New Year's Eve came. Glen and I celebrated at the restaurant, working the early part of the night cooking dinner for the masses, then drinking late into the night with our workmates. It was a new year, and I was starting a new life with Glen, although we had no plans for what was next. Glen had ideas about a wedding in the winter, with a horse-drawn carriage and long white fur cape to keep warm. This would make for a pretty postcard but was far from my ideal wedding. I'd hated the cold ever since my toes were frostbitten. Despite my lukewarm response, Glen continued with his vision, and I tagged along, just as I had with his dreams for restaurant ownership. My wedding would not be my own because I wouldn't speak my mind. I knew how to keep quiet to keep others happy and not rock the boat. I knew how to remain silent.

That's just what's done, isn't it? Don't rock the boat. Make sure everyone else is happy.

My birthday was coming up fast, and I felt tired and a little off. It was on my birthday at the end of January that I finally went to the doctor. He listened to my heart and lungs asked a few questions, including when I last had my period. I couldn't recall exactly. With the holidays, I had lost track. He did a pregnancy test, and when he came back into the room, I found out I was pregnant–on my nineteenth birthday. I would later joke that I was finally old enough to drink legally here in Canada, and now pregnant, I couldn't drink at all.

I went home, scared and completely overwhelmed.

I don't know anything about having a baby. My mom is going to kill me. I'm going to be in so much trouble.

I saw Glen later that day. "Glen, you know how I went to the doctor because I've been so tired lately. Well, it seems I'm pregnant," I said quietly, uncertain of how he might react.

"That's amazing. Wow!" he responded enthusiastically. He was twenty-four and seemed fine with the idea of being a father. We told his mother, who practically squealed with delight at the idea of being a grandmother. I did not want to tell my mother and delayed for almost eight weeks. It was March when I finally told her. Glen was over, and we were in the kitchen, standing around the table.

"Mom, I'm pregnant," I said and waited. She was quiet.

"You're what? You're pregnant? How did this happen?

You're on the pill," she said

"I don't know. The doctor thinks it may have been the antibiotics I was on over the holidays. Apparently, they can mess with birth control." At that time, we didn't have the labels on prescriptions that we now have warning of that particular drug interaction.

"There are options," she responded.

Glen couldn't believe what she was suggesting. "What do you mean? You don't mean..." he paused. "We aren't having an abortion."

That was the end of it. There was no further conversation. She peered at me with complete disbelief that I considered having a child with this man at nineteen. Abortion hadn't crossed my mind. I was engaged to Glen, and this seemed like a natural next step, albeit much sooner than I would have planned, not that I had planned anything. Of course, I don't think the reality of parenthood had entered my mind yet. When I found out I was pregnant, I read my mom's old copy of *Dr. Spock's Baby and Child Care*, which was seriously outdated. This was my only information about having a baby.

Within a couple of months, Glen and I had plans in motion. We started looking at apartments and secured one for August 1992, just over a month before our child was due. We shopped for living room and dining room furniture. We had Glenn's bedroom set for our room, and I had a dresser for the baby's room. We would get the rest of the baby things over the summer. Mom seemed surprised by the news of our move.

"What do you mean, you're moving out? How can you possibly do that?" she asked.

"What did you think I was going to do? Stay here and have

the baby?" I responded.

"But you need furniture and kitchen stuff. You can't possibly..." she trailed off in disbelief. I was a little stunned.

Had she not once in the last couple of years noticed the boxes of kitchen wares that filled my second bedroom closet from top to bottom?

She kept her extra sweaters and games on the shelf and had to have been in that closet dozens of times, if not more. The boxes were not hidden, with pictures of kettles and toasters visible if you just opened the closet door. This was the very same closet where I told her I used to hide the adult magazines her father once gave me. Yet even now, she didn't see what was right in front of her face.

"I've had everything I need for a kitchen up in my closet for more than a year. We ordered furniture, and it will be delivered to Glen's parents' place in a couple of weeks. We are moving on August first. We have a couch and chair, a wall unit for books, a dining room table, and side tables. I have my old chest that will make a great coffee table, and we have Glen's bed and our dressers. We need to get a few baby things, and we're all set," I said proudly, feeling so well prepared..

She stared at me blankly, not fully comprehending what was going on, her eyes filling with tears. Somehow, she hadn't realized that keeping the baby and being engaged to Glen might include us moving in together. She had no idea how proud of myself I was. Not only was I moving out, but we had found a beautiful apartment.

Moving day came, and we had the moving truck stop first to Glen's parents' house to pick up the purchased furniture and his stuff, then to my mom's house for my stuff. I was nearly eight months pregnant, so no one would let me do much of anything. Once in our new apartment, we assembled furniture and put everything away. I was finally able to unbox dishes and kitchen wares after being in my closet for over a year. The apartment had air conditioning and a dishwasher, both things I had never had before.

However, Glen said we shouldn't use the dishwasher to save on electricity, and so I washed things by hand. I also wasn't supposed to turn on the air conditioning, even though it was August and I was very pregnant. We needed to be frugal with our expenses. When Glen left for work, I unboxed some things and ran the dishwasher to save me from standing over a sink of hot water, dripping with sweat in the late summer heat. I even turned the air conditioning on for an hour or two but was sure to turn it off long before Glen was due home, so he wouldn't know. I didn't want to disappoint him. I felt bad that I was hiding this from him, but I also couldn't bear the heat. Hiding things brought up feelings of shame.

The first morning after we moved in, I set my alarm to wake up before Glen, even though I had started maternity leave early and could have slept in. I awoke early and promptly showered, did my hair, and put on makeup. I wanted to be the perfect little housewife. It was 1992, yet I had some 1950s image in my head of what I was supposed to do, and part of that was not letting Glen see what I looked like in the morning without makeup. I made Glen his coffee, set out his clothes, and worked on setting up our tiny apartment. When he left for work, I spent the day cleaning or getting things ready for our baby.

I had the idea that I could sew outfits for the baby and went fabric shopping. I asked my mom if I could borrow her sewing machine, and she agreed. I didn't want to face her because I knew she was still mad about me moving out, so one day while she was at work, I walked the few blocks and lugged the heavy old solid metal Singer sewing machine up the hill, back to my apartment. It was old and temperamental, and the thread would bunch up. I couldn't sew anything. I ended up buying myself a newer machine that was much lighter weight but felt guilty about spending the money, my money, without asking Glen. I sewed a few outfits and made little teddy bears that hung on the wall in the nursery. I decorated the room and washed and folded tiny baby outfits, waiting for this little human to be born.

Being the perfect little wife, I played house while my partner went off to work and came home to a hot meal and a clean house. I was the perfect little wife who felt she had to hide things, afraid to upset Glen. It was as though things had come full circle, and I was that four-year-old, playing house with my grandfather.

chapter 11

After settling into our apartment, I invited my mom and Glen's parents to see it. I was proud of the space we had created. Our parents walked up to the main entrance, and the doorman, complete with a tan uniform and flat-top hat with gold trim along the brim, opened the door and led them into the building. We had two regular doormen, and I came to know them well. Seeing them doing rounds throughout the building made me feel safe and secure. Looking out the window, I often saw Benson, who always smiled and waved up to me. As our parents entered, they seemed impressed by the marble floors, the posh furniture in the lobby, and the mirrored elevators. Glen's parents smiled and looked around while my mom seemed a little uncomfortable.

Once upstairs, Glen and I showed our parents around. The highlight for me was the washer and dryer in our apartment. There would be no trips down to dingy, dirty laundry rooms in a basement for me. The building had an outdoor swimming pool, a gym with lots of equipment, and a hot tub. It was elegant, and I was proud of the place I could now call home.

I had about five weeks in our new apartment to prepare before my daughter was due. I probably could have worked right up to the birth as I was not very big and didn't have any challenges while pregnant, but it was nice to start my year-long maternity leave a little early. Although there were no health issues with the pregnancy, it was a relief not to be on my feet all day long in a hot kitchen. I had no fears about giving birth. I figured I could take on anything. Despite my childhood, I still believed I could do or be anything I wanted, even if I wasn't sure what that would be.

A couple of the girls at work took up a collection to buy Glen and me a few baby gifts, and we had a lunch on the patio with co-workers as an impromptu baby shower. There was no family celebration of this pregnancy, even though this would be the first great-grandchild in the family. Nanny, however, did go above and beyond despite this. She knitted several baby outfits, sweaters, and blankets. It was the last knitting she did, as arthritis in her hands made it too difficult to continue.

Two weeks before I was due, the doctor told me that my daughter was breech and needed to plan a cesarian. I was incredibly disappointed, but the birth was scheduled for the next week. On Thursday afternoon, with my bags packed, I went for my last prenatal appointment before surgery the following day. We told our family to be ready for the news on Friday.

"Hmm. This is interesting," the doctor said while examining me.

"What? Interesting, good or interesting, bad?" I asked, a little worried.

"It feels like your baby may have rotated and might no longer be breech. Meet me at the hospital in half an hour, and we'll do an ultrasound,"

"And if she isn't breech, then what?" I asked.

"You go home and wait for things to happen naturally," he said, walking out the door. Sure enough, the ultrasound showed my daughter had rotated and was head down. It was unusual for a baby to move this much in the last weeks of pregnancy, I was told. I went home, relieved but also a little disappointed. I had expected to be having a baby, and instead, I'd probably be waiting another week, possibly more.

A week and a half later, on a warm September day, I had trouble sleeping. We still didn't turn on the air conditioning, and the apartment was hot. I rose around midnight, and for some reason, I decided I wanted to start making quilts, so I began drawing designs on graph paper with coloured pencils. I sat on a dining room chair, belly tucked under the desk, drawing and colouring for a few hours. I had at least ten designs completed before I eventually slept. The next morning, I woke up uncomfortable. I went through my usual routine, having a shower and putting on makeup, tidying the apartment, and having breakfast and a cup of tea. Mild contractions continued, but I assumed they were Braxton Hicks contractions that are uncomfortable but don't result in true labour.

Glen was home and slept in while I washed dishes and finished folding laundry. I double-checked my bag for my stay at the hospital, just in case this was the real thing. I went for a walk around the grounds of our building. When Glen woke up a few hours later, he came out and walked with me. Our friendly doorman kept watch and waved each time I passed by. It was a gorgeous, warm day, and I was in shorts and a long shirt. I walked and walked, occasionally pausing for deeper contractions, and started to believe that maybe this was the real deal. Glen and I headed to the hospital around 7:00 in the evening. It was the same hospital I was born in, an old brick building used primarily for birthing. The contractions had gotten much harder, but I could still walk around. When I was assessed, they said it would be several hours yet. They brought us to a room, and labour continued. Glen had gone to the cafeteria to get something to eat and came back with a tuna fish sandwich. I looked at him in disbelief. In the birthing classes, the instructor told us that the partner should not eat anything with a strong odour as it can be unpleasant for a soon-to-be mom.

"What are you eating?" I said with disgust.

"A sandwich. I'm hungry," he replied, bewildered.

"Tuna? Really? Of everything you could have chosen, you picked tuna."

"What? I like tuna," he said as he took another bite. I rolled over, trying to avoid the smell. Within a couple of hours, they offered an epidural, which I accepted thankfully. Once I had the epidural, I could no longer walk. The pain of contractions disappeared completely, and I fell asleep. Glen tried talking to me a few times.

"I'm tired," he said. I rolled over again, ignoring him, and slept through the worst part of labour. A nurse came in to check my progress, waking me around 3:30 a.m. She said things had moved along, and then doctors came in and told me it was time to push. This was a teaching hospital, and there was a young resident doctor attending. I imagined, being that it was early September and the beginning of the semester, he was likely early in his residency. This poor young doctor was pale, and I remember wondering if he was going to pass out. Glen stood beside me, holding my hand, but his hands smelled like grease from the restaurant and tuna fish from his late dinner. I pushed them away. The birth was quick and easy. Twenty minutes, with maybe four good pushes, and Ashley was born. I had my baby girl in my arms, tears rolling down my face.

Being only nineteen and in the hospital with my first child was an unusual experience. As it was a teaching hospital, new nurses were coming in and out, new doctors were reviewing charts, and there was a constant flurry of activity. The second day I was there, a student nurse, probably in his mid-forties, came in. He was supposed to assist with breastfeeding to make sure everything was going well. He was very hesitant and asked a few questions, although I had a hard time understanding through his accent and very quiet voice. He seemed almost timid. His supervisor, a sweet older woman, walked in and lit up the room. She was almost jolly and came over to show him how to check me for abnormalities in my breasts.

"Your milk is coming in wonderfully," she said, sounding very excited.

She showed the male nurse how to teach me to do a self-breast exam. He looked mortified that he had to touch another woman's breasts. I had no problem with any of it. Was it because I had no boundaries, or that by the time your baby is delivered in a teaching hospital, multiple nurses and doctors had seen every inch of me, so that one more touch is no big deal? The student nurses taught me to diaper, swaddle, and bathe my daughter while Glen returned to work. I guess the dads didn't need to learn this stuff, or maybe some dads stayed with moms in the hospital. Glen went home to bed then off to work. On day three, I went home. Glen and his dad came to drive us, and then Glen was right back at work, which was necessary as we had limited income. I was left all alone to care for this brand-new baby.

Two days after being home, I ran out of the pain reliever that I had been given at the hospital. I had a few stitches, received after the birth, and could hardly move without searing pain. I didn't want to call my mom because, somehow, asking her to drop off a couple of pain pills on her way home felt like too much of an imposition. I finally walked to the mall the next day with Ashley in a stroller to pick up what I needed. It was nice to be out of the apartment, although the days had that autumn chill. Two older women stepped onto the elevator at the mall at the same time as I. They looked at my tiny newborn daughter.

"How old is she?" they asked.

"Five days old," I replied, to which they were shocked at first. Then their faces softened, and it was like they witnessed a miracle. This tiny, brand-new human was in front of them. I realized later that in their day, they would have been in the hospital for the two weeks with a newborn, so this must have seemed strange to them. It felt good to see the joy my tiny daughter brought these ladies.

Ashley started sleeping from midnight to about 6:00 a.m. at about six weeks old, which was a sufficiently long stretch of time that I started to feel human again. I fell into a routine of caring for her, cleaning, and being the good little housewife, but I was unhappy and bored. I tried finishing my last English credit for high school, but it was so slow. I would complete a lesson and send it back by mail to be marked. The lessons I completed all received As, but eventually, it fell by the wayside as the demands of motherhood took over.

That year, I distinctly remember watching the World Series on television. We had basic cable, which did not include many channels, and it seemed that baseball dominated. I was never a sports fan, but Ashley was cranky and would only stop crying when I held her and walked. She wouldn't even let me sit. So, I watched a lot of TV. I stood with her in a baby carrier, ironing everything in sight, from blouses to sheets and cloth diapers, all while watching baseball for the first time in my life. Tom Henke would pitch for the Toronto Blue Jays, the first time a Canadian team had made it to the World Series in eighty-nine years. They won. It's funny how I still remember an event of no significance to my life in detail years later.

Glen would come home and eat, then fall asleep on the couch or go to bed. It felt like he wasn't around much, and I was very lonely. In all the time before and up to Ashley's first birthday, my mom came over to visit once. She lived only a couple of blocks away but didn't drop by. She didn't call. I know she was upset when I moved out. It would mean a lot of change for her. She would lose her subsidized family townhome, as the city saved those for families, and now she was living there alone. I also didn't make any effort to reach out to her. Nothing I would do at that time could possibly have made her happy anyway. I had dropped out of school and gotten pregnant. What could be worse?

The year passed, and maternity leave was over, so I went back to work. Glen and I worked opposite shifts to eliminate the need for childcare. Glen mostly worked days, and I worked a lot of evenings and Sundays. He would head to work in the morning while I took care of Ashley. Then around 4:00 p.m. I would catch a bus to work with Ashley in her stroller. I'd hand her off to Glen as his shift ended and mine began. I'd come home later in the evening and would give her a final feeding, then go to sleep around midnight most nights. Day after day, week after week, wash, rinse, repeat. Glen and I never spent any time together, and when he was home, he was usually asleep on the couch. He didn't put any effort into our relationship but wasn't any different than the years before. I had thoughts of leaving him, but I had no options. I would be a single mother with a baby and not enough money to live on my own.

How could I possibly work? Who would take care of Ashley?

Our lease was up on the apartment, and a co-worker had a house he offered to rent to us for a good price. We moved into a three-bedroom house and finally had space. I often missed my tiny apartment that was pristine and could be cleaned top to bottom in an hour. It had been an elegant apartment building with beautiful grounds, but now we had a small backyard and a home. This was the kind of place we were supposed to live in when we started a family. Maybe if everything was just right, Glen and I could both be happy. I loved the open concept and high ceilings. The finished basement could be a playroom when Ashley got older, and there was a full garage and a spare room for guests. The neighbourhood was safe, and there were primarily homeowners with just a few renters sprinkled through. It was very different from the tiny townhouse where I grew up with Mom. I was proving that I was good enough. Of course, a new house didn't change Glen. He was still absent, and our relationship suffered.

Back at work, I spent more time with the guys from the kitchen. Once Ashley stopped her late evening feedings, I no longer needed to be home early and often spent the rest of the night at the bar with the guys. The guys would hit on me, making me feel special. I was accepted, pretty, smart, and part of a group. My drinking was occasionally excessive, and there were a couple of times I didn't go straight home.

One night a co-worker drove me home. I was completely inebriated and barely awake. He decided he could take what he wanted, and I didn't know what was happening. He parked in an empty parking lot, climbed on top of me in the back seat of his car, and raped me. I didn't call it rape for many years, but I was unconscious or in and out of consciousness when it happened. This was most definitely not consensual, and yet the following day at work, he made a joke about it. I wasn't even sure it had happened until that joke. I blamed myself because I was the one who was drunk.

I must have wanted it. I must have been at fault.

I would only realize my self-destructive behaviour many years later. I would carry guilt and shame for being promiscuous and not being a good person for a very long time. None of the men around me, at work or at home, seemed to care about me, and I think I stopped caring, too. Neither Glen nor I put in any effort to change things, and I don't know that we would have known how had we thought to try. He smoked joints like cigarettes, and even when we were home together, he was almost always asleep on the couch.

One of the owners of the restaurant had always been kind, and we became good friends. He would often drive me home because, he said, it was on the way. Then one day, he pulled over, and he kissed me. In that moment, somehow, I was enough because this guy–no–this man wanted me. I was happy to go along with it. I was getting all the validation I ever wanted from this good-looking, smart successful man.

Why was it that Glen didn't pay attention to me?

Of course, I just went home and pretended as if nothing happened, secretly happy that I was desirable but unable to change anything in my life, or so I thought. The owner and I remained friends, but over time he stopped driving me home. He had a family and wasn't about to risk that on some young girl that worked for him.

I was rejected again. I had been, yet again, looking for

validation from any man who showed me any attention.

As often happened in our family, Mom and I swept our differences under the carpet and ignored them, but I still only saw her occasionally. Nanny had stopped hosting holiday family celebrations, and I would later learn that she had skin cancer on her back that she ignored due to her fear of doctors, and it progressed significantly. Despite all the past events with my grandfather, I still wanted to pretend like everything was okay. I had never wanted anyone in the family to know about Grandpa, so I chose to ignore it. I wanted life to be like I remembered as a kid when our family got together and enjoyed Christmas meals. I longed to return to the happy memories of my aunt's jokes that would have me rolling on the floor laughing or water fights that ended with my aunts ganging up on my mom and her being soaked to the skin. Our family gatherings were fun-filled and happy and were separate from my everyday life.

Now that we were in a house, I began hosting Christmas and family celebrations. I invited everyone. My grandparents never came. I was disappointed. I thought that Nanny didn't want to come because somehow, I wasn't good enough. My food wasn't good enough, my planning wasn't organized enough, and my house wasn't big enough or comfortable enough. Looking back, I can see this was the beginning of a major decline in Nanny's health. In reality, it had likely little to do with me, but that internal dialogue kept up.

Nothing you do is good enough. If you just tried harder, people would like you, and you could make things perfect. You have to do better. Status quo isn't enough. You need to work harder than everyone else because things don't come easily to you. There is always room for improvement.

Time was running out for Mom in her townhouse. She no longer qualified for a whole house to herself and would likely be moved to an apartment. Even with the government job she had started years before, she'd have trouble affording much on her own. The stable income and benefits meant Mom had stopped cleaning houses, and she had a great group of friends in the office. She seemed to be starting to enjoy herself and her newfound freedom. Occasionally, we would get together, sometimes visiting my aunt or taking the kids on a nature walk. Things appeared to have smoothed over between us.

When she needed to look for a place, we offered her our basement. It was finished, and she could have a bedroom down there. It seemed like a good fit, and we were happy to have help with the rent, even though Glen was making more money now that he had been promoted to kitchen manager. Having Mom around might be helpful. She rented a truck, and many of her work friends came to help us move her into our house, but with her now in just a bedroom, we had to store a lot of her stuff in the garage. We used some of her furniture, and she filled that small basement bedroom to the brim. Mostly, she was a quiet roommate and kept to herself.

Mom spent most of her time in her basement bedroom. She'd watch television and read a lot when she wasn't working. It was nice to see Mom with friends and going out. She was camping and going to parties, and it felt like she was creating a life of her own. I hardly saw her, as she was gone to work early in the morning, and I worked many evenings. By the time I was home, she'd be in bed watching television for the evening.

"Stacey, I thought I should mention something," Mom said one day. "A few times when I've come home from work, Glen has been asleep on the couch, and Ashley was in her crib screaming."

"What do you mean?" I asked.

"It wasn't like she had just woken up, and Glen hadn't heard her yet. He was dead asleep. I found her in her crib, her face red, and she had obviously been crying for quite a while," she said to me. I was ashamed of myself.

What do I do with this? I need to work. I can't talk to Glen about it. He's just going to sleep anyways. That's all he ever does. Why is he so lazy? Why does he smoke drugs? What can I possibly do about it? What am I doing wrong? Why doesn't he want to be better?

Glen and I didn't fight, but my resentment would grow when he didn't help out around the house. I didn't know how to ask for what I needed or wanted. I did my best to keep the house clean and the laundry washed, all while taking care of Ashley and working. I still wanted to be the perfect housewife, and perhaps, if I was good enough, everything would be okay.

Was I still trying to play house?

Then a day came when Glen told me, "I'd love to have another child. Wouldn't it be great if we had a son?" I wanted him to be happy, and maybe this would give him a reason to be home with his family and not high or asleep. I suppose there was a part of me that still held out hope that things could get better.

"Yes," I replied. What else could I say? It seemed like everything would fall into place. We'd have another child to round out our little family. I would get away from the restaurant and all the craziness there, including the drinking and staying out late. With a full year of maternity leave that I was entitled to, I could enjoy being a mom and spending time with Ashley and our new baby. It would be a chance to reset. I remember the day I agreed to have another child, and I know that was the night my son was conceived. A few weeks later, a home pregnancy test confirmed my suspicions.

Mom and I went to visit her younger sister and stayed late into the evening chatting about our lives and things going on in the world. My aunt and her partner loved talking about the most recent conspiracy theories, and I always found it interesting to listen to the stories. Later in the evening, the discussion turned to our family, and I casually mentioned that Glen and I were having another child.

"What?" my mom said, swiftly turning to me.

"I'm pregnant. I'm due next July," I replied, not understanding the look on her face.

"How did this happen?" She asked. My aunt shifted uncomfortably in the chair beside us.

"We decided to have another baby. The timing will work well, especially now that Glen is making more money," I explained.

"You planned this?"

We headed home soon after my news, and Mom didn't say anything to me the rest of the evening. The silent treatment again. It was a long, quiet drive home.

Thankfully, it was an easy pregnancy, as I was working even longer days because the restaurant was catering for the new NHL hockey team in town. Every home game, I would start work at 8:00 a.m. preparing food for VIPs and box seats, then around 4:00 p.m., we would head to the arena and set up for the evening. I usually worked until around midnight when we returned to the restaurant to clean up from the day. This happened three times a week for home games; then I'd have a week's reprieve when the team was on the road. That hockey season ran until early April. Our team didn't make the playoffs, so I could rest in my last few months of pregnancy and only work my usual eight-hour days. I stopped working in late June to spend a few weeks getting the house ready for our new baby boy. Unlike the apartment, the house didn't have air conditioning and yet, with nesting instincts kicking in, I found it necessary to clean the carpets in the early July heat and humidity on my hands and knees.

    The day came, and my contractions quickly intensified. Glen stayed home from work, and within a couple of hours, we headed to the hospital by cab. I was brought in and examined, but the contractions had eased, and they said I couldn't be admitted to a birthing room yet.

    "It'll be at least another day or two before this baby is born," I was told. "You can stay. However, we can't admit you until you are farther along. But there's no air conditioning in the waiting area. You might be more comfortable at home," the nurse told me. It was hot and stuffy, so I agreed to leave. It felt like staying would be an inconvenience to the nurses. Glen called a taxi, and I sat on the curb outside to wait, but the contractions started again. I thought about going back inside, but I already felt stupid for going too early. The cab ride home was long, and the pain was intense as contractions continued. We were home by mid-afternoon, and I spent the next hour watching the clock. Contractions became more intense, but I didn't want to ask Glen to head back to the hospital because I didn't want to spend the money on another taxi. If I could hold on until Mom arrived home, she could drive me. She would be home around 4:30 p.m. At about 3:00, I called her at work.

    "Mom, can you drive me to the hospital when you get

home?" I asked, a little out of breath.

"Yes. I should be home around 4:30," she said.

"I'm wondering if you can leave on time, or maybe even a little early," I said, straining through another contraction, not wanting to inconvenience anyone.

Daniel was born about an hour and a half after we made it to the hospital that evening, at the same teaching hospital where Ashley was born. However, the experience was very different. It was early July 1995, and perhaps it was between semesters for nursing students because they were far fewer people around. The night he was born, the nurse took my new baby boy to the nursery, and I was left in my room with the bed's safety rails up.

I remember lying there, needing to go to the bathroom. I pushed the call button as I had been instructed. "Your legs will be wobbly when you get up the first time after the epidural, so make sure someone helps you to the bathroom," the nurse had informed me. I pushed the call button again and waited. I stared up at the ceiling, listening to the sounds down the hall. It was so quiet, with only the sound of a door opening and the odd beep of some machine somewhere in the distance. I once again pushed the button. I didn't want to pester them, but I didn't know how long I could hold out with the pressure in my abdomen becoming uncomfortable.

Eventually, I gave up. I tried to lift the rail on the side of the bed but couldn't get it down. I pulled and yanked but nothing. There was a metal chair next to my bed, and so after getting on my hands and knees, I climbed over the rail, carefully stepping onto the chair and easing myself down to the floor. Apparently, the epidural had worn off sufficiently, and my legs were stable enough because I made it to the washroom without falling. I still couldn't figure out the safety rail, so I climbed back over and went back to sleep.

I had few visitors in the three days I was in the hospital, and Glen only returned when it was time for me to come home. Though he did have to work, the days were still long when not able to do much of anything but lie in bed. When I was ready to be released, Glen came with his dad, and we went home with our new little bundle. Glen burst with pride that he had a son. Then he went to work, and I was alone again, but now with a three-year-old girl and our infant son. Daniel was an easy baby and slept a lot. That was perhaps my saving grace as I did everything by myself in the house.

The owners of the restaurant where Glen and I worked were opening a second restaurant. I worked on the documents for the new menu, recipes, and training manuals, while he took on managing the new restaurant and planning the opening. The owners needed to replace Glen as the kitchen manager at our restaurant, and I was offered the job. I went back to work early from maternity leave in order to secure the position, which would give us more money and stability, and Glen's mom decided to retire from her retail job to take care of the kids for us. This felt like a blessing at the time. Maybe things would start coming together. We'd have regular care for the kids and could possibly take days off together for the first time. With both of us as managers, we'd have more money, too. Maybe everything would be okay.

Glen had made it clear years ago that he had no interest in buying a car or even getting his license. "There are too many idiots on the road," he'd often say. Even now, with two children, he had no intention of changing his stance. I knew then that he would never prioritize saving money for a car and gave up on the idea of ever having one. We ended up spending a lot of money on cabs, more than enough to have bought a brand-new car, but what could I do? I didn't even try to assert myself.

Don't rock the boat.

Glen's parents would come and pick up the kids before I left for work in the morning and then drop them off when I was done. Glen came and went as he pleased. I rationalized the behaviour as he was opening a new restaurant in a very busy location.

I started back in January with a kitchen where half the staff had been moved to the new restaurant. The owners didn't want to pay a little extra to get qualified, more mature cooks, so I was left with minimum wage staff who didn't want to be there. It was hell. I was training new staff and was in over my head. One owner would randomly fire staff he didn't like mid-shift, and I would have to stay to cover the shift. Nothing quite like finding out the owner fired the dishwasher at 5:00 p.m. on a Friday evening, just as I was about to head home for the day and then have to stay and wash dishes because there was no one else to do it. There was no concern about how their actions might affect anyone else at the moment. I didn't push back and set boundaries. I worked more and more hours, trying to keep labour costs down, spending less and less time at home.

Glen was also working long hours. We hardly saw one another, and nothing changed between us. There were no fights, but there was also no connection. I struggled with long hours and still maintaining the house with little help from Glen, but I thought I was being strong, holding it all together, keeping the house running, doing my job and taking care of our kids. This is what a woman was supposed to do, wasn't it?

I'd often start my shift before lunch and work over dinner, then stay around at the restaurant, do paperwork, and hang out with staff. Keith, who Glen had hired to replace me while I was on maternity leave, was often around. He was young, very attractive, and had a car which he saved for and bought himself. One night, I saw him sitting at the end of the bar struggling to do math homework, and I offered to help. Soon, I started tutoring him, sometimes at work, sometimes at home. One day, I caught him looking at me over his textbook, and he quickly glanced down, grinning, knowing he'd been caught but not actually caring. I was twenty-three with two kids, but he treated me like I was special. He'd drive me home after work, and he told me I was beautiful. Then one night, in that huge navy-blue Monte Carlo, our hands touched, and I looked at him, knowing that I couldn't resist anymore. He drove to a quiet spot and kissed me as I had never been kissed before. He caressed me gently, his hands moving softly over my body, and then made love to me. It was the most amazing evening I'd ever experienced. It wasn't just sex. It was so much more.

chapter 12

I knew it was wrong. I may not have been married, but I had two children with another man, and we still lived together. Glen and I hadn't been intimate in months, if at all, since Daniel was born. We'd occasionally pass each other at home for a couple of hours once or twice a week, but there was little to no relationship.

"How was work?" Glen asked.

"Same old, same old. I still haven't found any decent staff to replace everyone who went to your kitchen. They won't let me pay above minimum wage," I replied. Glen laid down on the couch, and with the remote in hand, within minutes, he was asleep. Great conversation. While on a steep learning curve in my new job, as I struggled to take care of the kids and the house, Glen spent more time at work, going through the growing pains of opening a new restaurant. I wondered about some of the staff he was spending more and more time with and whether he, too, was seeing someone. We didn't fight; we hardly even spoke anymore. We lived separate lives. My resentment grew with each load of laundry I did for Glen, with each bathroom I cleaned without help, with each dish I washed. Meanwhile, Keith continued to drive me home, and I helped him with his homework. He made me feel special and smart. He appreciated my efforts. He told me he loved me.

About a month later, I was at work preparing for a busy lunch. The phone rang behind the bar, and the bartender called me over.

"Hello?" I said, surprised to get a phone call so close to the restaurant's lunchtime rush. Anyone who knew me would know to call earlier or wait until later in the afternoon.

An unfamiliar voice said, "This is Ottawa Hydro calling. We need your consent to transfer the electricity bill to your name. We understand that Glen Nichols will no longer be assuming responsibility for the bills at this address as he has moved out," this voice said to me, very matter of fact. I looked out over the restaurant, starting to fill with lunch customers and hearing this person's voice but not really understanding.

"Excuse me. What did you say?" I asked, confused.

"You need to consent to take over the bill yourself and confirm that Glen Nichols will no longer be on the account."

"Um. Okay," I said, glancing across the parking lot outside the restaurant. What was going on? The bartender brushed past me with a case of beer to stock the fridge and looked at me curiously. I hung up the phone and walked to the back and into the small office. The tiny room with yellowing walls held two desks and hardly had room for the two chairs. I picked up the office phone and called home. Glen answered.

"I just received a call from the hydro company telling me you're moving out?" I questioned.

"My dad is here helping me get my stuff. I was going to tell you. I'll be done before you're home and will be out of your way," was all he said as he hung up. My mind went into overdrive. This was happening right now. Strangely, I didn't feel sad. A weight lifted from me, and my senses seemed more acute. I checked on the kitchen, and the staff were fine. I walked over to the bank across the parking lot and transferred money from our joint account to my account. I remembered my mom's story from when she left my dad, and he drained all her money out of the bank account. She was left with nothing. I left enough in the account to cover bills but ensured that my pay was safe. I didn't know what to expect from Glen and was not about to be caught off guard. I went back to work, allowing the busyness of the lunch rush to distract me. My mind ran through what had just happened, and then I realized that he wanted me to find out that way. He wanted someone else to break the news to me about him moving out. It hadn't been accidental as he would have had to provide Ottawa Hydro with my work number. He never confronted me or talked to me about our problems. He just packed up when I was at work and left. But then, it had been over for a long time. There wasn't anything to talk about, was there? We'd grown apart, and I don't think either of us was happy. Perhaps he was the one with the courage to take action and leave.

 That evening after the dinner rush, I headed home, not sure what to expect. Glen's parents kept the kids that night, and I entered a very quiet and empty house. He hadn't taken everything, but there were some definite holes. In our bedroom, our bed and his dresser were gone. I sat on the floor, looking at the peeling wallpaper left from the previous tenants. When the furniture was in the room, I hadn't noticed how much of that yellowing paper had lifted from the wall. My stomach was light, and my breathing was deep. I now understood what people meant when they said it felt like a weight had lifted off them. I was fine with Glen leaving. Maybe I had been hoping that he would go.

 With no bed, I slept in the living room on the couch my mom had brought with her. That old gold couch was the same one Chris had lain on so many years before when his abuse started. That couch had been in my grandparents' house, years before that, and now here I was back at the beginning, uncertain of my future, but somehow okay.

In the next few weeks, Glen's parents travelled back and forth between their house and mine, picking up the kids and dropping them off. I went to work, did my job, and went home. I was alone, but it felt good to have no one with expectations that I needed to meet. My mom still lived in the basement, but I hardly saw her. We were more like roommates than mother and daughter. As long as Glen's parents were babysitting, I could make this work. I could do it on my own.

A few weeks later, Glen came by my work, and we sat in one of the restaurant booths. He pulled out an envelope and counted out some cash which he gave me to cover a few bills.

"I think it's time I come home. We need to work on this and make things right," he said.

"No," I replied with a sense of confidence that I didn't recognize in myself, "It's over."

"Maybe we could try couple's counselling?" I half-heartedly agreed, but I knew there was no way I wanted to work on it. What was "it" anyway? It was not a relationship but felt like a swirling vortex of water, with me caught on the edge, fighting to keep from being sucked in and down. I was just going round and round, day after day, resisting that scary place. The relationship had been over for some time, and I had not felt so free, ever.

Glen tried his best to win me over. He asked to come over to the house, saying he had a few of my music CDs and wanted to drop them off, and of course, I agreed. He wanted to talk. We sat on the couch where he had spent much time napping over the years. It had been so long since we'd sat together on that couch.

I stared out the back window at the green space that extended behind our house. I didn't want to look at him.

"I love you, and I want us to get back together. The kids need us together, and I know we can get through this," he said. I studied him with uncertainty.

Was I making a mistake? Could I just walk away from the father of my children?

Glen leaned in to kiss me, and I let him. Of course, I let him. I always let guys do what they want. The kiss lasted a few seconds, and I pulled away. That swirling vortex that had held me so long was gone. I knew I had made the right decision. I was done.

"I'm sorry, Glen. I can't do this anymore. We just don't work together," I said through tears. I was sad, not by the end of our relationship, but by the hurt, we had both felt over the last few years. He left without another word.

I was at peace.

chapter 13

Life without Glen was freeing but presented many new challenges. Without a car, getting around with the kids was difficult. Anything I needed to do meant getting two kids dressed, then walking the few blocks to the closest bus that ran every half hour on weekdays and every hour on weekends. When Daniel was still small, I had to have the stroller, which was cumbersome to get on the bus. I would take Ashley up the steps and sit her at the front of the bus, then go back to the sidewalk and lift the stroller with Daniel in it. Some bus drivers were kind and would help, but many would look disgusted while they waited for me to get on. While my mom still lived in the basement with me, I rarely ever asked for a drive or for help. I was trying to be independent and prove I could do things on my own.

In our family, asking for help felt like a sin. It seemed like it was a source of shame to need help. Others may ask for money or groceries, but mom would take care of herself. It felt like those who couldn't were somehow "less than." I recall hearing the phrase 'pull yourself up by your own bootstraps' more than once. My mom and her sisters couldn't even accept things from one another. When they went out for dinner, if one offered to pay, the others would argue and secretly shove money into the others' purse to pay their own way, unable to accept kindness from another. Waitresses would walk away, shaking their heads, allowing them to argue over the bill.

Growing up with this attitude around not asking for help or accepting things from others, I realized that although my mom had a car, I don't remember ever asking her to take me grocery shopping with her. Many times, I would take a bus to buy two weeks' worth of groceries and then take a taxi home. It didn't cross my mind to ask her to babysit the kids so I could go out, especially since she worked all day and had friends. One day, I needed milk and decided it would be easiest to go to the corner store. I spent over half an hour working up the courage to ask her to watch the kids while I went for the ten-minute walk up the street. The kids were in bed, and she only needed to be in the house, but somehow, I had convinced myself this was a big ask. She said "yes," and it was no big deal. I sometimes wonder if I had asked more often throughout the years, I might have received more support, but I had built up walls and decided I had to do everything on my own without help. I pushed people out of my life because it was safer that way.

I had pushed Glen out of my life too, and now it had seemed his life was beginning to unravel. He left his job, or maybe he was fired, a few months after we broke up. He called me a couple of nights, feeling very low, and I'd talk with him, but I was not going to change my mind. I didn't feel guilty. I took responsibility for where my life was and expected him to do the same. Neither of us was really to blame. We just weren't a good fit anymore, if we ever were. With Glen unemployed and at home, I think his parents decided it was ridiculous that the kids were still going back and forth all the time, and so they suggested that the kids stay with them through the week and be with me on my days off. I was so tired, between working, parenting, and trying to figure out how to do it all on my own. It made sense to have Daniel and Ashley stay with them during the week. It would give the kids stability that I couldn't provide, so I agreed. I had no idea what Glen's parents had in mind. Glen said they would be by to pick up a few things for the kids.

The same day Glen called me about this new arrangement, he and his dad came to the house with their trailer attached to the back of the car. The kids were home with Glen's mom, and I decided to stay in my room, out of the way, as I didn't want to face them. My bedroom window overlooked the front of the house, and as I watched, I saw things being loaded into their trailer. They took all of Daniel's furniture from his bedroom. They had disassembled the crib, moved the dresser, packed all his clothes, and then they packed up Ashley's stuff—I was in shock. I didn't understand what was going on. As each piece of furniture was loaded up, I started to piece together the picture. They were removing my children. Piece by piece, my children's lives were being extricated from my home, and yet I stood motionless. All the weight that lifted from me when Glen first left came crashing back down upon me, and I crumpled to the floor. I was still not in control of my life.

I sat on the floor, back against the wall, tears streaming down my face. Tears turned into wailing as I realized that my kids were being taken, and I had no idea how to stop it. I had no choice but to go along with them because what else could I do? I couldn't stay home with them because I needed to work to make enough money to support them and myself. I didn't make anywhere near enough money to pay for childcare, so I was beholden to his family. The gut-wrenching sounds that emanated from within me were primal as I wept for the loss of my children.

I heard the car engine start, then Glen and his dad pulled away, and I was left alone in the house.

I walked to the bedrooms that I had decorated for my children. The teddy bear wallpaper border and imprints on the carpet where furniture once stood were all that remained in Daniel's room. Ashley's room had my old bed and dresser but little else. In the entire upstairs, the only furniture left was mine from my childhood bedroom--the bed where I had lined up my teddy bears and dolls around me, protecting me from the world, in the same bed where I cried myself to sleep so many nights, thinking there was something wrong with me. The dresser where I hid the bikinis my grandfather made me model for him. There were no bears or dolls to comfort and protect me anymore. I was on my own. I couldn't stand the sight of my children's empty rooms. I peered out my bedroom window, wondering if they had really left and if this had actually happened, but of course, the street was empty, and they were long gone. I wept, and then I became angry. I pulled at the edges of the old wallpaper on my bedroom walls, tearing large sheets off the wall. I ripped the pieces to shreds as tears and anger mixed within me. A piece of my soul was lost. Darkness came, and I lay in the middle of the floor, the empty walls and torn pieces of my life surrounding me until, eventually, I fell asleep.

Morning came, and I awoke, stiff from sleeping on the floor, head pounding from a migraine. I pulled myself up and into the shower, downed a few pain pills, and set about my day. I was robotic. I couldn't allow myself to feel because I would not have been able to move. I grabbed a garbage bag, cleaned up the shreds of paper, and threw them away. I washed the baseboards and vacuumed the little bits of leftover wallpaper, making perfectly straight lines in the carpet, creating a perfect pattern. It was as though I was removing every last memory of Glen. I closed the kids' bedroom doors, unable to face that emptiness.

Keith had kept his distance for the last few weeks. We talked a few times, but today I wanted him. I called, and he drove straight over. I laid next to him on the couch for what felt like hours, with my head on his chest. I could hear the distinct click in his chest. The first time I had heard it the month before, I asked what it was. I thought he had a watch in his pocket or something. Click, click, click, click. The soft sound of metal. Eventually, he told me that the sound was his artificial heart valve. He had surgery soon after he was born and again when he was twelve to correct his heart defects. He once told me, very nonchalantly, that he probably wouldn't live long since he smoked and drank, and the doctors had warned against it. I swatted at him.

"Don't be so morbid. You're young," I said.

Keith came over often, and I welcomed the distraction as I hardly saw my kids. Keith made me feel good about myself when I felt like a failure as a mother. Anytime I wanted to see them, I had to call Glen and usually, there was a fight that ended before arrangements for a visit could occur. I had no idea what to do or how to confront him. I had no money for a lawyer, and even if I got one, how could I make it work when everything was set up at Glen's parents with full-time caregivers?

While I was dating Keith, my mom also started seeing a man that worked in her office. They had both attended a co-worker's wedding, and that evening, she came home late and chatted with me by the front hall. I asked about the wedding and the reception, but she seemed distracted.

"Are you going to bed soon?" she asked.

"No. I'm not really tired," I replied.

She looked down coyly and said, "Well, I'm going out again." She was going to Tom's house for the night. After that evening, they dated regularly, and I saw even less of Mom as she was often at Tom's or in her room.

Occasionally, Glen would have his dad bring the kids over for a day or two. Daniel was getting bigger now and would climb out of a crib, so I put him on a toddler bed mattress on the floor, often in my room, as he seemed to sleep better when closer to me. Ashley still had my old bed and seemed happy to be in her own room still. One day she told me she never wanted me to move because this was her house. I decided then and there that I would do whatever I could to manage the rent by myself. I still had my mom paying a portion of the rent and eventually, I turned Daniel's empty bedroom into a spare room for a roommate. It was far from perfect, but I had to keep my house and give the kids some reminder of the stable life they once had.

Before too long, I purchased second-hand furniture for my bedroom. I painted the walls with some cheap mis-tinted paint from the hardware store, a deep plum colour that happened to match a wallpaper border I found on sale. Slowly, I began to decorate my space. The huge windows filled the room with light, and I had a few plants sitting on my dresser. There was space for a large desk where I started writing again. It had been a while since I had felt the desire to write anything. I bought the softest sheets I could afford and a fluffy down comforter to keep me warm when I was alone. It was a place where I was at peace when alone and loved fully and completely when I was not. Keith could touch me in such a way that I would tremble with passion. Never before had I been not only loved but also desired.

Keith often worked the same shifts at the restaurant with me and usually drove me home. As manager of the kitchen, I was far too lenient with Keith and let him get away with whatever he wanted. He was young and took advantage of the situation, and I was blind to it. This didn't help an already difficult situation, where the male cooks in the kitchen had trouble respecting a younger, female boss. The situation became worse, and the owner took me into the office. I imagine he offered to talk to me because we had been close, but it couldn't have been easy.

"I have to let you go. You haven't been keeping up with the work," he said. I couldn't believe it. I don't blame him now, but at the time, I felt betrayed. I was doing the work, but I was not a good manager. I thought the owner would have my back and, in some ways, I guess he did. He told me that he had spoken with a friend who owned a restaurant, and they would hire me. Perhaps he was kind because of his guilt over taking advantage of me a couple of years before, or fears that I would bring a sexual harassment suit forward, or worse yet, tell his wife.

I was devastated, wondering what I would do for money, but I was also tired of restaurant work and maybe a little relieved. There were no longer thoughts of opening a restaurant with Glen. That was his dream, and I was left with no vision for what my life might become. I had no idea what I wanted, and I had no dreams of my own. But I had to work, so I began applying everywhere except restaurants.

I was offered a job selling coupon books for local services door to door. My first day was a nice fall day, and I enjoyed being outside walking. The first few houses, I listened to my training partner to learn the sales spiel. After a couple of doors, we split up, and I started knocking on doors by myself. For many, there was no answer. Occasionally someone would answer the door, and about halfway through the pitch, they would say, "No, thank you," and close the door. One door opened, and there in front of me was a girl from high school.

"Hi, Stacey," she said kindly.

Oh god, she remembers me.

I gave my pitch.

"No, thanks," she said, looking at me with pity, "but it was great to see you." I slunk away, feeling worthless as I tried to sell stupid coupon books that no one wanted. I kept at it that day, and in the evening, after a quick dinner break, we went back through the same neighbourhood, trying the houses where no one was home earlier. It was a long day, and since I was training, I only received half of the commission for the sales I made. My twelve-hour day ended, and I was exhausted.

They seemed surprised I came back for a second day. It seemed that most people didn't stick it out. I needed to give it a fair shot, but after spending another twelve hours knocking on doors, my commission for the day worked out to a whole twenty dollars. It had been cold that day, and in the coming weeks, it would only get colder. It was hopeless. I hadn't told Keith about this job because I was ashamed of how miserably I had failed. The next day, I stayed in my warm bed and decided to give up on my door-to-door sales career.

A few weeks later, I had an interview at a retail store that sold men's suits and casual wear. When I walked in, I figured I was in way over my head. I knew nothing about suits. The only suit store I had ever entered was when I took Glen to a high-end store and bought him a suit, tie, and dress shirt. At the time, I didn't know there were cheaper places we could have gone, so

Glen got a $1,000 suit in the early nineties. Despite my lack of any experience or knowledge about men's wear, I was hired by the end of the day. I later learned that the full-time guys liked to hire young girls to work in the store. It was good for business and their sales quota. I wore dress clothes, heels, and nylons to work every day. Having worn jeans and t-shirts for the last several years, I didn't have much money for clothes, but I found a few fantastic pieces at the local thrift store. Our store's tailor would alter my suit jackets when she had spare time, and I ended up with essentially custom pieces that I still own today.

The environment was so different from the restaurant, where I would leave feeling greasy and grimy. Now I had sore feet after a long day in heels, but I felt respectable and could go out without needing another shower. Keith often picked me up after work, driving that old Monte Carlo. The other girls in the store commented on how cute he was, with his blonde hair, blue eyes, and chiselled features. He was thin and well built but not a big muscle-bound guy. To me, he was perfect. By the following spring, Keith was finishing his first year of college and talking about moving in with me. I wasn't getting a lot of hours at work and could use the help with rent, and he was ready to move out of his parents' house. We loved each other and were ready to take that next step.

Even though I was working only a few days a week, Glen's parents still kept the kids on most days. The holidays were a nightmare. If I wasn't nice to Glen on the phone, he would say I couldn't see the kids. Two days before Christmas, he threatened not to let me see them. I was crushed. He did relent and let them come over Christmas Day. They were supposed to be at my place by 10:00 a.m., but of course, it was well after lunchtime before they arrived. Every interaction with Glen seemed to end with a fight. Phone calls ended with me slamming down the phone, sometimes throwing it across the room. Glen was unreasonable, and what I wanted didn't matter. It was his and his parents' way or no way.

My anger grew, and I sometimes wouldn't speak with Glen to avoid a fight, but it meant sometimes I didn't see the kids. I had no idea how to change the situation. I thought of taking the kids back full time, but I didn't even know where to begin to make that happen. I had very little income, and I didn't have the support Glen had, living for free with his parents, who paid for everything.

How could I compete with that?

I did the best I could, but it never seemed like enough. In my mind, I had abandoned my kids, and that was the guilt I would hold for a very long time. I went on as best I could, missing my kids, thinking that the only way I would get them back was if I went to a lawyer. That would cost thousands of dollars, and I hardly had enough to pay for food and rent. One month, I pulled out an old tin I had with change and rolled nickels, dimes, and quarters in order to pay the phone bill. Somehow, I always managed to find the money to pay whatever was most pressing, but there was never any extra to spare.

It was the end of April when Keith was writing his last exams for school. The plans for him to move in were coming together. Once the semester was done, he could work full time and help pay rent. On the morning of his last exam, he went to school early and left me a note saying that he was going out with friends from school that evening and would take me dancing the next day. We were celebrating one year together.

Saturday arrived, and I didn't have work, so I spent a leisurely morning at home. I showered, had a late breakfast, and waited for Keith's call. I knew he had planned to stay out late with his friends, so I was not surprised when I didn't hear from him.

Mid-afternoon, the phone finally rang, but it was not Keith. A voice on the phone said he was in the hospital and someone was coming to pick me up. The voice on the phone spoke, but everything sounded muddled. I didn't understand anything except that his uncle was coming to pick me up. I don't know if ten minutes or an hour passed, but a car came, and I was driven to the hospital. Keith was in ICU, and the nurse led me to his bed. I picked up bits of the story. He had gone out with people from school and stayed over at his best friend's house. They woke up the following day, but Keith didn't. His friend noticed something seemed off and tried to wake him but quickly realized he wasn't breathing. He called 911. The paramedics came and were able to get his heart beating, but he had not regained consciousness. I sat by his bed, with nurses coming in and out and family and friends circulating. I barely noticed who was there. I was there two days, refusing to leave. I would not go home. I only drank some cold tea. Those two days were one long blurred stretch where I occasionally rested my head on the side of his bed, drifting in and out of sleep a couple of times. I held his hand and talked to him.

"You're going to be okay. You're going to get through this." I even talked to God. My beliefs had always been scattered and uncertain, but at that moment, I had nothing and no one else to comfort me. "Please, God, just have him move his hand a little or his eyes." I thought I saw his eyes flutter, but the nurse explained that it was just a reflexive movement.

They've already given up on him. What can I do? Is there anything I can say to make them wait and give him a little longer? This can't be happening. This isn't real.

There was a meeting with the doctors, his parents, brother, and me. The tests all came back, showing he was brain dead. There had been no activity, and it was time to make the decision to stop life support. I said nothing. I just sat quietly, going along with whatever they said.

Don't rock the boat. This isn't your choice to make anyway. You have no voice here.

Later that day, we gathered around him as the nurse came and began turning off the machines keeping him alive. They said it could happen quickly. I held his hand, the tears streaming down my face once again, urging him to make a move and prove them wrong. Just a twitch. Anything to let them know he was still there. But it never came. He was gone.

Keith's family drove me home, and I walked into that empty house. No children, no Keith, not even Glen. I assumed my mom was there somewhere in the house, although I hadn't seen her in days. I was utterly alone. I walked up the stairs without turning on any lights, passing by my children's empty rooms. It didn't seem real. I wanted to turn around, and see Keith walking up the stairs behind me, or maybe he would be waiting for me in my room. There was no one there. I showered, the warm water washing away the two days of hospital smell, sweat, and tears. I didn't even bother washing my hair, and as I got out of the shower, it hung, tangled and wet. I fell asleep, huddled in the fetal position, unsure how to go on. My mom checked on me once to see how I was, and I said I was okay. I lied.

The next few days were a blur. Keith's parents included

me in the funeral preparations and allowed me to help with decisions about what he would want. I went back to their home for a meal with several members of the family. I had the chance to sit in his room and take in everything. He was everywhere in that room. His clothes still smelled like him. I laid on his bed and pulled the sheets and covers around me as if he was still there. I held a box with a small gold chain; I had bought it for him for the anniversary we would never celebrate. I asked that the funeral home put it on him for the service. I spoke at the funeral, although I have no idea if any of it was coherent. They played his favourite Pink Floyd song, "High Hopes," which I picked and turned out to be much too long and painful to listen to, but there we were, sitting in pews listening as the song went on and on. He loved that song. Maybe eight and a half painful minutes were what I wanted, to truly feel all the pain that was bottled up inside of me. I wanted to fall down that deep, dark hole of despair.

chapter 14

The weeks after Keith's death, I existed within a fog. My mom's boyfriend, Tom, was worried about me and gave me some money to tide me over. He knew I wasn't working and was completely broke. I slept a lot but eventually climbed out of bed and went back to work. I didn't interact with customers much in those first days at the store. I unpacked boxes and re-stocked shelves. I organized ties on the display table and straightened the suits hanging up. I made sure the sleeves hung evenly in a row, and the sale tags attached to the cuff buttons were straight. The store looked like a picture from a catalogue. When certain songs came on the radio, I would stare off, lost in my thoughts. As one of the girls working with me would notice my mood, the song would suddenly change. I did not break down crying but rather became a shell of a person, just going through the motions every day.

When the kids did come over, we watched movies, huddled in the living room, eating pizza and ice cream. They loved it. We watched more Disney movies than I ever knew existed. Disney movies always had happy endings, and I was content with a little escapism. Having been off work for a while, money was tight, so Glen would drop off some food when he brought them to me. I think he felt sorry for me. I was humiliated that I hadn't even gotten food for the house. My own pathetic existence repulsed me. Some days I told Glen not to bring the kids and that I was working, but I would stay home in bed all day.

What did I have to offer these kids?

I had nothing left inside of me. They would be better off without me around.

One evening, when the kids were safe with their grandparents and Glen, I lay in bed with a migraine pulsing through my head. I took a couple of painkillers. Then I took a couple more, hoping they would help me sleep. If I took enough, I wondered if the sleep would be so deep that I wouldn't wake up again. I took a few more pills.

The kids don't need me, a useless mother who can't take care of herself, let alone them.

I took some more drugs. I don't know that death or suicide were on my mind, but rather, I wanted the pain to end for everyone. I wanted *this* life to end, not specifically *my* life. I didn't know what else I could do.

I called Glen to tell him that he wouldn't have to fight with me anymore about when I saw the kids.

"What did you do?" he asked.

"I took some pain pills. Well, maybe a lot of them. I just want to sleep now," I said, tears welling up.

"I'm going to call 911," he said

"No. Don't do that," I begged. I was mortified that someone would know what I had done. So I dragged myself to the bathroom and managed to make myself sick. It was the only way Glen had agreed not to call anyone. "Please don't tell anyone," I begged him again, "I'm okay now, honestly," I told him I would be fine and hung up. I went to bed, drained and exhausted.

The next couple of days were hazy. When I awoke, the world was spinning, and I went back to sleep. I was unaware of my surroundings and probably lucky my liver didn't shut down. I had taken close to fifty pain relievers and missed work. I called a day later to apologize. They were very understanding and probably assumed I was grieving. My mom assumed I had a migraine and left me alone. Migraines were always a great way to hide whatever was going on in my life, and yet again, the lie worked.

Within a few days, I managed to pull myself out of bed, shower, and get back to some semblance of my life, however, empty it still felt. There was nothing left in my life. The bus I took to work would pass the cemetery where Keith was buried, and I would stare out the window, feeling like a bubble surrounded me. I was angry at people on the bus who were going about their lives like nothing was wrong.

How can they act so normal when Keith has died? Don't they know the world has forever changed? Don't they see that nothing can ever be the same again? Why are they so happy?

My empty days went on, one after another, the tide of grief washing over me several times a day.

Slowly, there were fewer moments of intense grief, and I started to come up for air.

Maybe I won't drown.

I managed to keep working part-time and somehow got through. Money continued to be a challenge, and my account was in overdraft most of the time. Lily, an old friend from the store, was looking for a place to stay because she had broken up with her boyfriend. I needed a roommate, and she was a good friend. It was perfect. She moved in, and things seemed to be looking up. Time passed, and slowly, my grief lifted. I started to see the light at the end of the tunnel.

My co-worker, Clark, had always been kind to me and

mentored me in sales. He was about twenty-five years my senior, and yet I trusted sharing my inner thoughts with him. He boosted my confidence, telling me I was pretty and smart. He encouraged me at work and drove me home some days. One day I got a call from Glen saying Daniel was in the hospital. My heart stopped. I was at work, and it was closing time on a Sunday. It would take me hours by bus to get across town to the children's hospital where they had taken him. Clark offered to drive me. He did small things like that for me all the time.

On our way home one day, he told me his daughter was a realtor, and he asked if we could make a stop as he needed to check on one of her empty listings. He suggested I come in with him for a few minutes. We walked to the kitchen of the house, and he took my hand. He led me to the living room and leaned down to kiss me. I hadn't felt anyone's arms around me in some time, and it felt strange. Then Clark began to undress. He pulled a condom from his pocket, and I realized that he had planned this encounter.

He kissed me again, and a vision flashed before my eyes of my grandfather. My grandfather had kissed me like this. Clark's five o'clock shadow brushed on my cheeks, and I was frozen. I couldn't stop him. I was numb and couldn't wrap my head around what was happening. He was like a father figure to me. I couldn't insult him; I didn't want to upset him. I did what I had always done and simply went along with it. He penetrated me, and I lay motionless, trying not to feel anything. After a few minutes, he was done and dressed. I pulled my skirt back down and straightened my shirt, and then he drove me home.

I never said anything. I had let him kiss me. I never said no. At work over the next couple of weeks, he made more and more suggestive comments. He wanted me to meet his friends and planned a trip to his cottage. He bought me my favourite perfume, something I couldn't afford for myself. Eventually, I started to make excuses for not getting driven home and avoided him as much as possible. Lily and I were going out more, and I enjoyed being free for the first time in my adult life. I was getting to experience what it was like to be truly on my own.

A few weeks later, Lily and I were having a party at my place. A few people arrived early while my mom was making dinner. Around 6:30 p.m., the doorbell rang, and there was Clark. He had taken a taxi and had a small bottle of rum in his hand, almost empty. He was weaving and slurring as he spoke.

"What are you doing here?" I asked.

"I heard there was a party," his words slurred as he pushed past me. My mom offered him coffee, and he sat down heavily on the kitchen stool, slurring more incomprehensible words. His tone grew louder and angry.

"Time to go home, Clark. We are having some people over, and I need to get ready," I said.

"I know. That's why I'm here. For the party. Why didn't you invite me? I had to hear about it from someone else." He was angry.

"This isn't your kind of party, Clark. A bunch of young kids drinking. You wouldn't have any fun," I said, standing up and walking toward the front door. My mom stepped in and suggested he leave, so he followed me. Then in the front foyer, he stopped and turned around.

"It's time to go," I snapped at him. He wasn't leaving, so I pushed him toward the door. He got louder and more aggressive. He resisted, but then fell. I stepped over him and grabbed him by both arms, dragging him out the front door. My small five-foot, 100-pound frame somehow dragged this six-foot-tall man. His forehead caught on the door latch and was gashed deeply. The blood dripped across the front step and onto the concrete as I continued dragging him outside. He stumbled his way down the concrete stairs and took the small glass bottle of rum he had tucked inside his jacket, drank the last of it, and smashed it on the driveway.

Someone had called the police, and they arrived to see him standing on the street, yelling at me. The adrenaline pumped through my body, and I stood firm. The cops stood between us, and one asked me a few questions, while another spoke to him. I was on the front steps and could see him maybe twenty feet away, glaring at me. He didn't move. I was too mad to be frightened. I didn't care what he did or said. The two cops conversed briefly and then came over to me and said they would take him away. They asked if I felt safe in my home since he seemed almost obsessive.

I stood—strong, almost invincible. "I'll be fine."

I was not putting up with this kind of shit from any man again. I was never going to have a man control me or have power over me—ever again.

PART 3
resolve

chapter 15

After that, something shifted within me. Lily and I went out to bars and danced until the lights were turned up to let everyone know it was time to leave. We even drove an hour and a half to Montreal one evening to enjoy the nightlife there, getting home slightly before dawn, in time to sleep a couple of hours before heading to work. I dated several guys and had fun. I didn't want any serious relationships, and I didn't need or want a man in my life. There was no one to control me, no shame hanging over me, no fears of consequences for things beyond my control. I was on my own, and I was enjoying it.

Lily became my greatest cheerleader and support. If Glen resisted letting me see the kids, she would drive me over to his parent's house and stand behind me as I confronted him. Lily loved the kids, and together we went on vacation, taking them to the huge amusement park in Toronto. She helped me buy new furniture for their rooms, and we painted the walls in bright colours. She injected life into the house and helped me shed the misery of so many years.

My mom still rented the basement from me and had been working for the government for a few years. When she came home and asked if I'd be interested in a job, I agreed and was hired for a temporary position. Surprisingly, it was quite nice carpooling with mom to and from work every day. I saw her far more than I had in the last several years. At work, we would talk about whatever was going on in the world. Somehow, Lily and I still managed our crazy evenings out until 1:00 a.m., and then I would be up and ready for work at 7:30 the following day. I did well at the job and tried to learn as much as possible. Mom was hard on me at work, feeling like she had to be sure no one thought she was showing me any favouritism. No matter what needed to be done, I did the work without complaint. I learned all aspects, no matter how boring or repetitive. There was a competition for a permanent position a year later. At that point, I had learned enough to come out on top, and I was hired. I finally had a stable income with benefits.

One of the girls I worked with was looking for a place to live. By this point, my mom and Tom had been dating for a while and had hinted at the idea of living together. The timing seemed perfect, so my mom moved out to live with Tom, and my new roommate moved in. Our household was now three young women and a cat.

I had a few other roommates over the years. One roommate left behind a few belongings, including a self-help book. I read the book and started to understand how my past had affected my thinking. I didn't absorb it all, but it opened me up to new ideas and ways of thinking. I was starting to see the possibility of a new life.

Work was busier as we approached Y2K, and the government needed to prepare for potential computer failures and the resulting mayhem on infrastructure. Amidst the fears, there was also a sense of joy. With the coming New Year, everyone planned parties to celebrate the new millennium. Lily and I had made friends with a local bar owner and planned to ring in the New Year there. Ironically, this was the same bar that Glen and

I had gone to several years before on our first date. Now, I was close friends with the new owner. The evening was to be the start of something new. A new start, not only to a new year, decade or even century, but a new millennium.

Yet, for Lily and me, it was uneventful. The most exciting part of the night was when we went to a friend's house after the bar closed and couldn't get a taxi. We walked down the middle of a snowy four-lane street at 3:00 a.m., in long evening gowns and high heel shoes to the house several blocks away. I went home the next day, and it felt like any other day. Little did I know that things would all change a week later.

Even though I had a stable government job, I was still afraid of not having enough money, so I had kept my part-time job at the menswear store. The following Saturday, there was a boring corporate dinner at a restaurant to celebrate the end of the busy holiday season. Lily and I decided to have our own party for our friends from work. By this time, Lily was managing one of the store locations across town and had hired a young guy named Stewart. The evening of the party came, and Stewart arrived straight from work with one of the new employees, Kevin. They were both still in their suits and ties. I had only spoken to Kevin once on the phone to get some merchandise transferred to our store. His deep dark voice was sexy and caught my attention. He had black hair and piercing brown eyes that softened when he laughed. His smile was warm, and he laughed as we all sat, drank, and talked about work, books, and music.

Kevin had only agreed to come to the party because another girl he knew was supposed to be there. Luckily, the girl never arrived, and Kevin stopped asking if she was coming. Several times that evening, I caught him looking at me. We were a large group, crowded around the living room, sitting on couches or the carpeted floor. With his back against the bookcase, he looked very handsome in his dress shirt. The suit jacket and tie had come off at some point in the evening, and his shirt sleeves were rolled up. I brought him a beer and sat beside him, saying nothing. I listened to the conversation amongst our friends and realized he was intelligent too.

When Kevin went out to the garage to have a cigarette, I joined him. I didn't smoke but wanted the opportunity to be alone with him. I was back in high school, shy and afraid to be too close, but wanting to make some move to show I was interested. I brushed my hand against his. He didn't return any gesture, but he sat next to me for the rest of the evening when we went back inside. We talked late into the night. Several people crashed at our house, and I assigned a few guys to sleep on the couches. I told Kevin he could sleep in my room but that we would be sleeping; I had to work early the next morning. A few of his friends seemed surprised as he followed me up the stairs. We lay next to each other and talked for another hour. We shared a kiss and then went to sleep.

It was the first time ever that I didn't feel the pressure for more from a man.

chapter 16

Kevin and I began dating and were inseparable. We saw each other three times that first week, and then almost every night after that. I was taking a few university courses, and Kevin and his friends would play music at the Tuesday night jam session at the university bar, Rooster's. After my evening class, I would sit and watch him play guitar and on the very rare occasion when he would sing. When Nicole said she was moving out a few months later, and I was worried about paying rent, Kevin suggested moving in, especially since he was already there most of the time. Even though we'd only been seeing one another for four months, I agreed. It seemed almost too easy. I knew Kevin was serious about moving in when he brought his prized possessions—his guitars—to the house. He was here to stay. It was almost hard to believe.

I was dating this astounding guy who wanted to live with me, had a job, and would contribute to the rent. He was clean-cut, didn't do drugs, and was smart. He was opinionated and appreciated our debates when I disagreed with him. I could be myself and have my own ideas that were different from his. We spent almost every moment together, going out or staying home. I finally gave up my job at the menswear store, feeling secure enough with my permanent position. Kevin and I spent many evenings discussing politics, religion, the many books he was reading, and the courses I was studying. That year I took a psychology class, and it piqued my interest into how the human mind works.

A year passed and my old landlord gave us notice that he was selling the house, and I had three months to be out. I worried about where I would go, but I knew things would be alright. Kevin and I began looking for houses and finally bought a small but beautiful townhouse with gleaming hardwood floors and a curved staircase to the bedrooms above. We chose a three-bedroom house so that when Ashley and Daniel came over, they each had their own room. I continued to take university courses, hoping to better myself. I knew education was important, and I had a vague idea that it would help me at work.

December of 2001 proved eventful. A week before Christmas, I was out shopping for gifts and took a taxi home. The taxi couldn't get around the bend on our street as fire trucks were blocking it off. I walked around the bend and stood at the end of our driveway, shopping bags in arms. My knees buckled. There was a ladder across our garage, and our front door was open. Firefighters ran past me, and I stood confused. One came over to me and walked me back to the edge of the street. The neighbours had a fire, and it had threatened to spread to our unit. They had broken through the door to check for fire in the walls, but we were lucky. They had large fans running to clear the smoke and possible carbon monoxide in the house. I told them I had a cat, and they went into the house to search for Kitty.

I called Kevin at work, but the girl who answered the phone said he had left. I told her that if he returned to the store, have him call me immediately as there had been a fire. Then I called my mom, and she had Tom drive over.

I actually asked her for help!

The firemen had found Kitty, and I gave her to Tom to take home for me so she would be safe. I waited and eventually was given the all-clear to go into the house. Our unit had been spared. It smelled of smoke and burnt plastic, but otherwise, you could hardly tell anything had happened. On the outside of the house, the siding was melted, and the outer pane of the dining room window had cracked from the heat. Minutes after I was allowed in the house, Kevin walked in. I ran over to him, and he held me. It was scary, but we were fine. I felt safe—and protected.

A week later, on Christmas Eve, we came home to our little townhouse after spending time with Kevin's family. I was blessed that we still had a home, unlike our neighbors, whose house had to be gutted and rebuilt. I changed into PJs and sat admiring the lights of the Christmas tree. Kevin poured us a glass of wine, and then he sat next to me. He pulled out a small box and said, "Will you marry me?" I teared up, not believing this was happening. We had talked about marriage, but I wasn't sure Kevin was ready to make that level of commitment yet.

"Yes!" I replied and kissed him. He later told me that he had been with his best friend buying the ring the night of the fire. They had gone to celebrate and have a drink before he stopped back at work to pick up his stuff prior to heading home. The girl in the store told him our house was on fire. He told me he rushed home and that when he came home and found me, he almost gave me the ring that night. I was glad he waited. Christmas has always been my favourite time of year.

Unlike in past relationships, I voiced my opinions about what I wanted, and Kevin listened. Best of all, Kevin was great with my children, Ashley and Daniel. Things had settled into a good routine with the kids coming over every weekend. Kevin helped take care of them and supported me through the usual parenting struggles. I was thrilled at the prospect of this man being a stepfather to my children. He was a good man.

Right after we were engaged, I came down with chickenpox. It was terrible, and I was off work for three months with complications. At a time when I should have been planning my wedding, I was sick. I was cranky all the time, and we later joked that if we made it through that, we could make it through anything. Wedding planning waited until Spring when I started to feel better. We didn't have much money, and we did many things ourselves. We made the décor and printed our own invitations. My mom seemed happy with this relationship. She liked Kevin. She even offered to address all our invitations by hand in calligraphy.

The wedding was simple in a downtown church where Kevin's family had often gone to mass. We rented the basement hall for our reception and had a great party. We left two days later on our honeymoon through New York State, with three nights in New York city, and then worked our way up the coast through Connecticut, out to Cape Cod, Boston, and Maine, before heading back home. It was a whirlwind trip. One evening in New York, we dressed up–I in my long black gown with my hair up and Kevin in his dark suit. We went to dinner at the Waldorf Astoria. At the restaurant, a couple at the table next asked to take our photo. They wanted a picture of true New Yorkers. We laughed to ourselves, coming from Ottawa, Canada, but I was pleased to pass for a New Yorker that night.

We settled into our new life together. I was working for the government, and before long, Kevin was promoted to assistant manager at the store. He was a natural leader and a kind, caring, person. He was hitting his stride in his career, and it felt like we had more stability in our life.

Children were important to Kevin, so we talked about whether it was a good time to start a family together. At thirty years old, I didn't want to wait too long. Kevin's mom said, "There's never a good time to have children." That helped us decide to start trying. I got pregnant immediately. We told our parents, and everyone was happy for us. A few weeks later, I miscarried. But before I had a chance to stop and think, I was pregnant again. I sometimes feel guilty saying I became pregnant so easily, as I know many struggle. Then perhaps, maybe it was my turn to have something come easily to me. I learned how to handle challenges and had weathered many before. This felt like a small bump in the road.

With our growing family, Kevin and I decided it was time to look for a bigger house, and just two months before our baby was born, we moved. No one would let me touch a box on moving day, but as soon as they were gone, I set about unpacking and making our new house into a home. This was a difficult year because while there was so much joy in our lives, we also had our difficulties. Kevin's father was diagnosed with cancer and died a few weeks before our daughter was due to be born. While Kevin and his father always had a complicated relationship, I think a grandchild may have given them a second chance, but it was not to be.

The obstetrician I saw for Ashley and Daniel was still practicing, so it seemed logical to go back to him. Things were very different this time, though. Kevin came to all my appointments and was involved in every step of the pregnancy. Unfortunately, the doctor was not wonderful. When he would enter the tiny exam rooms that we were herded into, he would completely ignore Kevin, like he wasn't even there. The doctor had years of experience, but he had minimal bedside manner. Luckily, when it was time to go to the hospital, he wasn't on duty, and we had another doctor.

I had decided to attempt natural childbirth, but the nurse kept asking me if I wanted nitrous oxide to ease the pain. I kept saying no.

"Can I get it set up for you, just in case you change your mind?" the nurse asked, and I agreed, mostly so she would stop asking. Little did I know, this meant bringing the tank of gas beside my bed and putting the mask in my hand. She instructed me to hold the mask to my face and breathe in to relieve pain. Let me say that when I was mid-contraction and had a mask with gas in my hand, it was hard to resist. Kevin was right beside me, rubbing my shoulders, holding my hand, and asking me what I needed. I ended up using the mask a little throughout the hardest contractions, and, as with my first two, when it was time to push, nothing was stopping this baby from coming.

"Wait. We need to get the doctor," the nurse said with a straight face. I almost laughed. This baby was coming now, whether she liked it or not. The doctor rushed in, still putting on gloves, as Lauren was making her entrance into the world. It was over in a few minutes, and we had a baby girl.

We were thrilled to bring home our baby girl, and I found such joy watching Kevin as a parent for the first time. Lauren was the first grandchild for Kevin's mother, and she helped a lot over those first years. I had been a little worried about having another baby and all the responsibilities and sleepless nights, but Kevin was a hands-on father and shared in everything that needed to be done.

Lauren was just over four months old when my Nanny died. The skin cancer she'd ignored for several years progressed until she was in a nursing home. I visited her once with my mom in those last days. Nanny sent my mom to get her some juice. I stood beside Nanny's bed, looking down at this frail woman who was once a powerhouse. She took my hand and said, "I'm sorry." Her eyes closed, and she went back to sleep.

Mom and I left that day, and I never saw her alive again. I've often wondered what she was sorry for, but I imagine it was about the things my grandfather did to me. It had been fifteen years since I disclosed what my grandfather had done, and for the first time, I heard an apology. The apology would not come from my grandfather, who died a year later, but from the woman whose opinion mattered to me most. My only regret is that I didn't spend more time with her in those last years, but perhaps that's how she wanted it. She didn't want people to see her diminished by this awful disease, and my memories of her will forever be of that woman who was strong and persisted through so much trauma of her own. She made a life for herself and worked hard to be sure they were cared for. I hope that if she saw me now, she would be proud of me.

A mere six weeks later, death would visit our family again. I got an unexpected call from my step-brother-in-law, someone I had never met. He had taken on the challenge to find me, as my dad was in the hospital and hadn't kept track of any contact information for his only daughter. The man on the phone said my father would like to speak with me.

"Hi, Stacey. I wanted to talk to you. I'm not doing well," he said. He had cancer. On one of their annual trips from Arizona back to Canada, he felt a little off. He went to the doctor, and within a few weeks, he was in the hospital with lung cancer that had spread to his brain.

"I'll come and see you," I said.

"There isn't time," he replied.

"I'll be there within the week," I replied, and then I planned a trip to see my father for the last time. Kevin, and Lauren, a mere six months old, came with me. When I arrived at the hospital, I had no idea why I was there or what to say. I wasn't even sure why I went, except that it felt like I needed to be there. The first two days, he was still able to talk a little. I introduced him to his granddaughter. I went to the hospital every day but one when his wife, my stepmother, encouraged us to go and see the mountains, a short drive from the city. I think she wanted to spend some time alone with her husband. By Friday, he was unconscious, and I stayed with him while his wife took care of a few things. I sat by his bed, holding his hand. His breathing was laboured, and I kept saying, "It's okay. You can let go now." About ten minutes later, he passed peacefully.

The funeral was planned for Monday, but my return flight had already been booked for Saturday. I was invited to stay, but the people at this funeral were a part of his life that I didn't know and who didn't know me. I decided to leave as planned. I had said my goodbyes, and there was nothing left for me to do.

Six months later, when Lauren was about ten months old, I found out I was pregnant again. It was strange how a year filled with so much death also brought new life. This time, we didn't go with the same doctor. Since I had already had three children, we felt that a midwife would be a safe alternative. We were planning on delivering at the hospital, but before the end of my pregnancy, we were so comfortable with the midwife that we ended up having a home birth.

A warm evening in May, my contractions began. We called the midwife to give her a heads up and called my mom over in case we needed someone there to watch Lauren. I tried to sleep for the night and may have slept a little on and off, but I was ready to have this baby by early morning. The midwife came early and predicted he would be born by 7:00 a.m., but, of course, as babies have a mind of their own, Joseph decided to take his time and wasn't born until noon. It was a completely natural childbirth, and right after, a tremendous surge of energy swept through me. I was ready to take on the world. This feeling persisted for a long time afterward. This experience gave me a newfound confidence.

The next few years were a blur of sleepless nights, crying children, flu bugs, diaper changes, and everything that goes with having two babies only eighteen months apart. As with many marriages, Kevin and I had our low points where we didn't always connect, but somehow, we always came back together, stronger than ever. There were months when it felt like we hardly spent time together without a baby or toddler climbing on us. Luckily, Kevin saw the disconnect. One day we had a long talk, and I saw that I was wrapped up in being a mom and wasn't putting any attention on our relationship. It was a slow start, but we made a point of connecting at least once a day in some meaningful way. I even set a reminder on my phone to pop up every day at 7:30 p.m., telling me to connect with my spouse. By that time of day, the kids were usually in bed, and we could sit and chat or watch a movie together. As the kids started sleeping better, we were even able to bring more intimacy back into our lives.

We managed to bring routine and stability into our days.

Before long, my maternity leave ended, and I headed back to work once again. One day the Director General for our sector called me to her office.

"You should finish your degree now while the kids are young. Once they get a little older, you'll be busy with all their activities, and without a degree, it will be hard for you to progress in your career," she advised. The thought of school felt impossible. I was only just starting to feel human again, and now I was going to add the insanity of school to the mix. Kevin and I discussed it, and as always, he was supportive and encouraging. I decided I could make it work.

I had taken a couple of classes at the local university the year before I started working for the government and had continued taking one here and there. Still, now I was being encouraged to finish. Work was supportive and gave me the flexibility to leave during the day for classes and then come back and work in the evening to make up the time. I took one class every semester and then tried doing two. I was almost always the oldest student in the classes, and one semester had an evening class taught by a man who also worked in the government by day. He told me that the day would soon come when I would see the light at the end of the tunnel and would want to fast-track the last few courses to get that piece of paper—finally. He was right. A year later, I found myself taking a full-time course load of five classes while working full time, with a family to care for and a house to manage. I have never worked so hard in my life. I sacrificed any free time to finish my schoolwork and still have time with the kids and Kevin.

I will always remember the day Kevin said to me, "I admire you." Three little words that were a jolt of pleasant surprise. We were sitting in the bedroom, getting ready for bed, and I was overwhelmed with emotion. This smart, good-looking, amazing man admired me. I knew for sure I had someone in my corner, someone cheering me on. But there was more to that moment. I saw myself as someone that others could admire. I accepted the words and felt good about myself.

My last year of school was the hardest. The fall semester, I was plagued by a case of C-difficile, brought on by some strong antibiotics I'd been given a couple of months prior. The symptoms are very nasty, and I have no idea how I continued working and going to classes. On top of this, I had started a new job within the same department, and while it was fun, it came with a steep learning curve. Kevin cared for me when I was home, drove me to doctors' appointments as we tried to get the C-difficile under control, and took care of the kids so I could concentrate on school and work.

Kevin would often take the kids out on adventures so I could spend Sundays working on papers and assignments or studying for exams. Finally, in the Spring of 2010, I finished my last course. Someone told me when I finished my last exam to stop and take in the moment. I recall putting down my pen and looking around. I had no assignments due, no readings to finish, and no more exams to study for. I was all done. I could walk out to my car, completely free of all school obligations. The moment was surreal. I stood up, handed in my exam, and walked outside. The sun was shining, and the rays of light streamed all around me, lifting me. It had taken thirteen years from the first course to the last, with a pause to get married and have two children, but I did it. My degree was finished. This was a huge milestone, as I had never graduated from anywhere. There had always been a sense of shame when those job applications asked for your highest level of education, and I never had anything I could check off. Now, I could check the box next to an undergraduate degree.

The day I graduated, Kevin said to me, "You're good at this school thing. Maybe you should go back and get your master's." I didn't want to think about more school. Instead, I focussed on work and my personal interests. A few years before, I had started following Jack Canfield, the author known for the *Chicken Soup for the Soul* book series. Now I had time to devour his work, including his book, *The Success Principles*. I started to see myself and a career I might build. I formed a vision for my life. I created a mastermind group that met every two weeks, helping each other move towards our goals, and I took a coaching certification course to start helping others. Day after day, I saw employees working for the government who were unhappy and counting the days to retirement. I knew people could be happier, and I wanted to help them experience more, enjoy more, and be more. That became my motto.

Coaching was rewarding, but some clients had challenges beyond my knowledge base, and I looked for ways to learn how to help them. Even though I had only been out of school two years, I filled out an application for a master's degree in Counselling Psychology. Now, I had to wait to see if I was accepted. That same summer, the opportunity arose to go to the seven-day seminar, Breakthrough to Success, with Jack Canfield. I jumped at the chance. I boarded a plane all by myself and headed to Arizona in August. The idea of going by myself was frightening. Some of the negative self-talk floated in my mind. It was unbelievably hot out, but the hotel was spectacular.

The first morning, I walked up to registration, and there were crowds of people around me, hugging one another and smiling. Many of these people obviously knew one another. I felt awkward and out of place. I was scared that I had made a huge mistake. When the doors opened, three hundred people gathered and listened to Jack speak. We spent the next seven days together, and I learned more about myself in that one week than I had in the previous decade. I decided to be open and vulnerable. I decided to be completely honest with myself. I saw the obstacles I had faced and how to break through them. I recognized my own patterns, and best of all, I discovered the dreams that had been within me all along. I created a vision for my life and had an action plan to move forward.

Halfway through the week, I was checking my email when I saw the one I had been waiting for. I was accepted to the master's program. I think I froze for a moment, in shock that I would be back in school a month later. I quickly called Kevin and gave him the news.

"I knew you could do it! Congratulations," he said.

"You know, I could never have gotten to this point without you. You have been my rock and supported me through it all," I replied.

"You did this all on your own," he said, and I realized he was right. The week of self-discovery ended on a high note, and I knew that I could be proud of myself.

I loved Jack's work so much that I went back for another seminar that fall and again two years later. I was now two years into the master's degree—and overwhelmed. I had all these fantastic goals, yet I couldn't execute them. I was still in school, already burning the candle at both ends. Then, synchronistically, I sat with Jack at the final dinner reception.

"I have so many goals and plans, but I don't know how

to fit it all in. There are just not enough hours in the day. I'm already working full time, in school full time, and have kids and a husband at home," I told Jack.

He looked up from his dinner. "You don't have to do it all at once," he said. A simple idea, not so very profound, but to this day, it rings through my ears whenever I feel like there's too much to get done.

Despite the challenges of my childhood and early adult years, my life was on track. It may have taken longer than I would have imagined, but I was finally doing things that mattered to me. I had a voice and could make decisions for myself. I was the mother I wanted to be. While I knew I could do it on my own if I had to, I didn't need to. I had a loving partner who I could trust completely and who would support me through it all. I no longer had to live with secrets hanging over me, worried about judgment and pain. I could—and I would—continue to be persistent in whatever I was doing.

I might not be able to change my past, but I could change my future. Truth be told, I don't know that I would change my past. It has brought me to this place, and I am happy.

EPILOGUE

I started writing this book a dozen times, in different formats and as fiction and non-fiction, never sure where the story would end. Of course, that is the funny part. The story goes on, but the book has to end somewhere. I am currently sitting here, during a global pandemic in 2020, wondering what the next few years will bring. I have come so far, and it can feel like there couldn't possibly be more, but then life turns around and surprises me.

As with most things I have done, finishing my master's degree took longer than I would have liked. The last obstacle was finding a placement to do an internship, but at long last, I completed the Master of Arts in Counselling Psychology program in August of 2017. My internship supervisor decided to take a leave of absence from the centre where she worked, and we ended up sharing an office for a year and a half, setting up our private practice. As I built my practice, I saw more clients and rented my own office. I now have my very own space, decorated just the way I like, and I did it on my own. I am now spending my days helping people overcome things like anxiety, depression, and childhood sexual abuse.

I think back to one class in particular where we learned about the different psychopathologies. It was January, cold and dreary, and I was tired and burnt out from the holidays and month after month of classes that felt like they had no end. I read about pedophiles, and suddenly, I had the word for my grandfather. I always knew that what Chris did was sexual abuse, but I didn't have a word for my grandfather's behaviour. I curled up on the floor next to my bed and cried. My grandfather was a pedophile and what he did was not okay.

My experiences have helped me to help others. My clients don't know my complete history, although there are parts that I've shared to let them know they are not alone. I love the work and love my clients, but as I have approached the end of this book, I long to spend more time writing, so I can reach more people by developing programs and writing books. I also long to stretch that creative writing muscle and write some fiction, hopefully with stories that will inspire, inform, and educate.

My mom and Tom bought a house out on the Ottawa river and now enjoy beautiful sunsets from their back windows. Mom and I have grown closer. I have come to realize everything she had been through and how she was a victim in this story as much as I. We talk on the phone regularly, and we go out for barbeques at their beachfront property. She and Tom take in rescue cats and always seem to be nursing one back to health or taking in an older cat to spend their last years in a home where they are loved. Mom seems to be content with her life, and while I know she still struggles sometimes, she has her dream house in the country, by the water and someone to share it with.

My oldest daughter, Ashley, married her childhood sweetheart. They moved to Switzerland for his job, where Ashley enjoys the small European cafes with friends and has started taking dance classes and learning German. While it is challenging having her so far away, I am glad they have this opportunity to explore Europe. They took a train, arrived in Italy in just hours, and experienced weekend trips to Paris. I am proud that she took the leap of faith and moved across the world to live her own life.

Glen's parents both passed away within a year of each other, and this left his family in a bit of turmoil. Glen ended up in a small town on the Saint Lawrence River near the Canada-US border, with his new wife, while his sister cleaned and cleared the house to sell it. With the house being sold, my oldest son, Daniel, moved in with us. Had you asked me a year or two earlier, I would never have thought this would be possible. From about the age of sixteen onward, our relationship had been strained. The long-lasting effects of the move to his grandparents when he was a baby made it difficult for us to maintain a close relationship. When they died, he was twenty-three and had not known life outside of their home. He was grief-struck and not in good health but within nine months, he was taking better care of himself, going to the gym, and working. It has been great having him around. I feel like I have been able to make up for some of the lost time and have been more of a parent to him this last year than I was in the past. I think our relationship has healed tremendously.

My daughter, Lauren, plans to go to medical school even though she still has two years of high school left. If I know Lauren, she has enough persistence and determination to do whatever she sets her mind to. She is a good teenager, and we talk openly and honestly about almost everything. I have no illusions that she keeps things from me, but I don't think there's much. One day, she told me about her friends and some of their struggles. She turned to me and said, "Mom, I don't have any trauma. It's so weird." That was a moment I will remember for life. My daughter has escaped childhood without anything traumatic happening to her and is growing into an awesome, young woman.

Joseph, my youngest, will be the hardest to watch grow up. He is my last, and I now understand why parents have trouble letting go when their last child leaves the house. His growing up marks the end of a very long era of parenthood that started almost twenty-eight years ago. He may be taller than me now, but he will always be my baby. He is a sweet, caring individual that I know will do something special in his life. We share deep conversations, and he makes me laugh with his sense of humour. I look forward to seeing the human he will become and the impact he will have upon this world.

Then there's my husband, Kevin, who's done better than I could ever have imagined. He has done fabulously well at work. From his early years in retail, he has kept moving up and has built a great career in business. His success has meant I no longer worry about paying the bills. He has been there, supporting me when I opened my private practice as a psychotherapist. Building the practice has taken longer than I thought but taking my time has allowed me to grow into this new role and a new career.

My relationship with Kevin keeps getting better. There are still challenges, and yet, somehow, we seem to keep coming out the other side even closer and stronger as a couple. When I do couples counselling with clients, I often realize how lucky I am to have such a fantastic partner who truly loves me and supports me. Like many, being stuck together in the house during this pandemic every day, all day, has tested us as a couple. The one marked difference is that we have learned how to communicate better over the years, and as our relationship has evolved, we trust each other in ways I would never have thought possible. So many men in my life hurt me and made me question my worth, but Kevin raises me up and supports me, showing me that I was right to believe that there are good people in the world.

For a couple years, I had a photo on my desk of the main

castle at Disney World with fireworks cascading down around it. That was a dream trip, but I had no idea how to manage it. Well, the day came, and we went to Disney World. As we walked up Main Street, I saw the Cinderella Castle, and tears rolled down my cheek. My mind raced back to that four-year-old watching the Wonderful World of Disney on Sunday evenings, hoping for my fairy tale ending. Maybe dreams can come true. Maybe there are happy endings.

As I sit in the newly outfitted library in our beautiful house, I look out at the backyard, complete with a pool. I guess I finally got that pool my dad offered up almost forty-three years ago. I marvel at the life we have created. I am astounded at how far I have come. Sometimes, I still struggle to be proud, as the fears of unworthiness can creep in now and then. Most of the time, I can accept that I have worked hard and made some good choices that have brought me to this place in my life. I am happy with the person I am today. If the past events got me here, then it was worth it, no matter how difficult they were to endure. Our greatest strengths come from our greatest challenges.

The abuse and poverty I experienced as a child had an effect on my life, but I made a choice not to let it hold me back. It hasn't been easy. Even today, I continue this journey of healing and forgiveness with my therapist. He told me to be gentle with myself, and I try. I've set my expectations high, but I know I don't have to do it all at once. I can allow myself to take my time and work through each day at my own pace. No one else is keeping score. There is no crowd cheering me to the end of the finish line. This is my journey, and only I can decide which is the right path.

I am happy that I have a life where I can give back and

hopefully leave the world a little better. As chair of the board for Voice Found, an organization that works to prevent childhood sexual abuse, sexual exploitation, and human trafficking, I can take my experiences and help guide programs to help countless others avoid some of what I went through. I want something good to come from my past, and I believe it can.

Lastly, as I write the closing words of this book, I can be proud that I have finally fulfilled a commitment to myself to share my story. I have always wanted others to know my story, but the reasons have evolved. Early on, I wanted someone to know and help me. Then I wanted people to understand my choices. Now, I want people to know they are not alone, and there are people who care. I want to give people hope that they can take their experience and grow from it, allowing the trauma in their life not to pull them down but rather give insight and a foundation upon which to build.

I try to live my life with intention, and I now have my own dreams. I say what I think and do what I want most of the time. When I don't, I recognize it very quickly and course correct. I need to live my life with my purpose in mind. I need to feel like I have given back because that is my choice. People can no longer take from me, and, therefore, I am at ease giving of myself. You won't likely see me with a glass of milk and cookies, but most days, I can be found either with my clients in therapy or sitting writing—and always with a warm cup of tea beside me.

ABOUT THE AUTHOR

Psychotherapist Stacey Kirkpatrick's life was filled with trauma however her journey is proof that healing is poosible, and that life can be what you make it, even after being raised by a single mother in the projects and being sexually abused by her mom's boyfriend.

Stacey is a co-author in the International #1 Best Seller, *Women Who Impact* and now, in *Milk and Cookies: An Intimate Story about Rising Above the Trauma of Sexual Abuse* brings you the story of her childhood where the experience of sexual abuse and trauma were as commonplace as milk and cookies.

In her private practice, Stacey spends her days with clients who struggle with the effects of sexual abuse and other mental health challenges. She also volunteers as Chair of the Board for Voice Found, a charitable organization that works to prevent sexual abuse, sexual exploitation and human trafficking. Stacey has a Masters in Counselling Psychology and studied personal development and transformation under Jack Canfield. She lives in Ottawa, Canada with her husband and is mother to four children.

www.ingramcontent.com/pod-product-compliance
Lightning Source LLC
Chambersburg PA
CBHW070149100426
42743CB00013B/2858